Structured For Success

Structured For Success

J Richardson

iUniverse, Inc.
Bloomington

Structured For Success

iUniverse books may be ordered through booksellers or by contacting:

iUniverse
1663 Liberty Drive
Bloomington, IN 47403
www.iuniverse.com
1-800-Authors (1-800-288-4677)

ISBN: 978-1-4759-1020-9 (sc)
ISBN: 978-1-4759-1023-0 (ebk)

Printed in the United States of America

iUniverse rev. date: 08/25/2012

CONTENTS

INTRODUCTION

This book is a tool to assist pastors and church leadership devise a ministry structure plan for their churches. It is not an all-inclusive plan. It can, however, serve as a guide for the pastor and his leadership team, within the church, to discover the following:

> How God's given purpose is accomplished. Each church needs a sense of purpose. They also need a well developed mental picture of their future for purpose to remain focused and assist them to know when they are winning or losing. If you were playing on a basketball team, how would you know that your team is winning? Obviously you would look up at the scoreboard. Well the church needs to have an effective structure in place to help them know when they are winning or losing.

> Secondly, to discover the countless ways a church may use to arrive at its destination. Also learn what components are necessary for the church to be successful in its quest as well as discover the climate that is conducive for this "vision odyssey".

> Thirdly, learn what the church should look like in the vision process. Will it be found in a state of integrity with all of its core values in tact? Will the church remain focused on its future?

> Finally, discover how to evaluate your church's accomplishments during the vision quest. Learn how to grade quality in the areas of excellence, objective success and goal setting as well as program completion.

When I went through the Police Academy in Florida, we were taught in firearm class to aim at the bulls eye of our target. We also learned the importance of the sight portion of our firearm.

Positioning and careful aim are critical to successfully hitting the mark. The bulls eye was the point of reference. The sight helped in the process of accomplishing the objective, which was to hit the bulls eye.

A ministry structure plan will help the church discover and remain focused on its reference point or purpose. It will also assist you define and document the purpose of your church or mission statement.

This statement will aid, as the church's purpose, in accomplishing its vision. The end result is that you will discover what God has called you to do and successfully obtain your pursuit in expanding the kingdom of God.

Structure is like the Center of Operations for the church's living being and doing. It enables the life of the church to excel and facilitates its ministry and missions. Structure is similar to the central nervous system of the human body. This system sends out signals to the brain which in turn gives the commands to different parts of the body to perform certain functions. In essence this is what church structure does; it ensures that each ministry is supported and the Great Commission mission is carried out properly.

Therefore, every church needs to write the vision, the structure, and the plan. They need to make it plain and run with it in hand. The leader must wait to hear from God, receive the vision, write it out, make it plain, and give it to the runner in order that he or she can move out with the vision in hand and tell the people of God.

It is essential that every church understands the necessity of vision and that it comes from God.

Before we can begin to run, we need to know where to run and what to run after. After we receive God's vision, we need to run with it in hand. So, when you read it, when you hear it, run and tell it. Run and shout it from the mountaintop! Many times, we start running before we hear from God.

Reach for the vision, grab hold to the vision that the Lord has laid out for your church. In order to grab hold to the vision that the Lord has for your church, change must come.

The word change comes from the Greek word "metanoia". This is where we get our English word metamorphosis, which means to be transformed. A caterpillar has to be willing to give up what it has always been so that it may become what it is suppose to be—a beautiful butterfly. A tadpole must be willing to change, if it wants to become a frog. In order for a tadpole to become a frog, it has to lose its tail and grow legs.

For the church to fulfill its purpose it must be willing to let go of the old and grab hold of the new—a new church, a new ministry, a new adventure, a new vision. To experience God to the fullest, you must be willing to change.

Grab hold to God's vision, His purpose and run with it!

CHAPTER ONE

Something to Think About

First, the church must have a clear strategy and vision of where God is leading them. They must be able to determine what is important. Once the church knows what is important, they will be able to clarify the wins, as they do ministry and serve the congregation and the community. Structure assists the church in discovering the best way to accomplish the win and the right steps in getting there. The church should have a strategic plan to discover their vision and purpose. This will allow them to carry out the Great Commission and outline a clear path for the church to get where God is leading them as well as find out where God is working and join in with HIM. There are two steps for this:

Step One: the *foundation* for strategic planning; leadership must be ready, willing and open to change.

Step Two: the *method* for strategic planning; the church will have to dig deeply, pray diligently and seek God fervently in order to discover the vision, purpose and core values of the church.

A church should have a good structure in place; I call it structured for success. Structure provides boundaries as well as assesses how the church's being and doing of ministry is carried out. How a church does ministry is the doing. The being is how the church goes about doing its ministry. It also gives a church the means and ways to operate with a smooth flow throughout the ministry.

A successful church will need to come up with a designed structure that will help their organization to operate effectively and efficiently to advance the kingdom of God.

There should always be an understanding of the Church's purposes to establish the best practices necessary to accomplish the ministry that has been set forth for it to do. The structure design will ultimately enable the church to do what God has called it to accomplish.

Each church should have its own Unique Fit. Every church is different from any other church therefore, it's structure has to be the right fit to carry out the vision God has given you.

Leaders must be empowered to lead. They should be given the tools they need to lead, trained how to lead, and encouraged as they lead. Leaders should be taught to have a team approach when it comes to serving within their ministry. Helping them learn how to work interdependently and not independently is vital to team success.

Every leader should be encouraged to have a leadership strategy, objectives and possess leadership commitment.

Every leader is to be passionate about their calling and the contentment that comes with that calling. Most of all a great leader should have the character traits of a caring spirit, a disciple's spirit, a supportive spirit and a giving spirit.
There are four steps for this;

Step One: *Personal Leadership;* God has called us to be His ambassadors. *One* must experience transformational leadership to think and lead like Jesus.

Step Two: *Interpersonal Leadership;* how we interact with others.

Step Three: *Team Leadership;* leading by personal credibility and trust.

Step Four: *Ministry Leadership;* is our approach to ministry as well as being able to coordinate the interaction of various ministries to achieve the church's goals.

The church must understand that the Pastor should have permission to lead as God directs him. The pastor's leaders should understand how to lead from a second chair role, while the pastor leads from a first chair role.

CHAPTER TWO

The Pastoral Leadership Mandate

Communicate to the leadership and membership the importance of putting God's purpose for the church in action in accordance with God's standards. This must be accomplished as written in His holy Word.

Allow God's Word and its principles to be the authority as you seek God and determine what His vision is for the church He has called you to lead.

This is only a model to give the church structure and accountability, from a team concept. It is a reflection of the Jethro Model as found in Exodus 18.

The Pastoral Leadership Team has a grave responsibility—to help the church carry out her mission and define her priorities. They will also assist the pastor in leading the church to the next level that she will move from being a good church to becoming a great church. This is accomplished through dreaming, re-dreaming, rethinking and reevaluating the vision, purpose, core values and ministries of the church as well as enhances and enrich the fellowship of the church.

It is essential for the pastor and his leadership team to spend much time in prayer both corporately and individually. It is also important for them to have an authentic team spirit and the same goal in mind, which is to expand the kingdom of God. This leadership team must leave personal agendas outside, and bring an attitude of love and fellowship to the church.

Making a Impact in the Lives of Others

It is my experience that passionate leaders are able to influence a change in the attitudes of the people they serve. This will result in a better environment, to learn, worship and serve God in. There are several steps which will increase a leader's impact. First of all the leader must understand the Life Wheel to make a significant impact on those he or she serves.

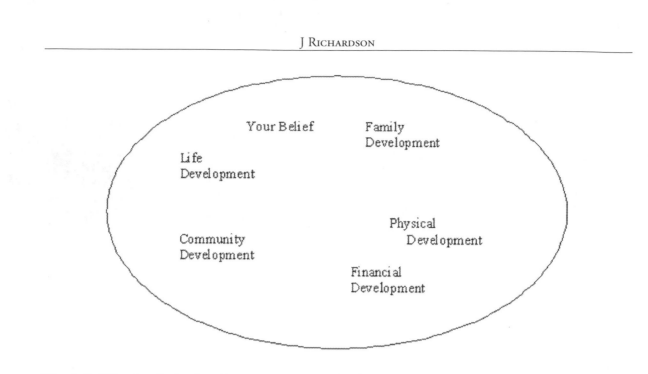

The Life Wheel will, firstly, allow you to set goals, discover priorities, as well as empower you to accomplish the impossible and maximize your effectiveness for the kingdom of God.

Secondly, passionate leaders should understand who God is. God is the absolute authority in the church. It's not the pastor or any leader, it is God. Passionate leaders will understand that the church is the product of God's transforming power. God calls leaders to assist Him, through the power of the Holy Spirit, to make an impact upon the world as well as the church. Leaders are mandated to positively influence the attitudes of individuals resulting in a better people. A better people will create the optimum environment for worship and fellowship. Passionate leaders will always be advocates of change. The reason the church is stagnate may be because it continues to stay the same. Why? For the simple reason, people refuse to change. There was something interesting about the early church. They adapted to the culture they were ministering to. When you are with Jesus, change should be happening everyday. The reason the church is not transformational in its scope, is because the people who make up the church are not changing.

Martin Luther King wrote some 40 years ago, from a jail house in Birmingham, Alabama, "If the church today does not recapture the sacrificial spirit of the early church, it will lose its authentic ring, forfeit the loyalty of millions, and be dismissed as an irrelevant social club with no meaning for the twentieth century." Today the church is losing its identity. Reggie McNeil in his book "Present Future" says the church has a case of mission amnesia. It has lost its identity." He also stated that the "church is on life support." In other words many churches are struggling to survive.

Thirdly, a passionate leader should understand who he or she is. We must remember that we were created in His image. Therefore, one of our responsibilities is to make God visible to a lost and dying world. A passionate leader will follow the example of Abraham. God called him to leave his country and go to an unfamiliar place. It was a path of faith. He found it and then he followed it. Sometimes it means taking a risk. In order to move beyond mediocre, one must be willing to follow God's paradigm shift. He instructed Abraham to do three things;

1. Leave his country. This for us may mean a change from the norm. There was revelation from God and a response from Abraham. His response symbolized a step of faith and a trust to follow God.
2. Leave his relatives. Natural affection must make room for divine grace.
3. Leave his father's house. Leaving your comfort zone to follow God's will and way. When God calls, we must be willing to leave behind those things that are dear to us and a constant temptation. Abraham's country had become idolatrous and his father's house was filled with an ongoing temptation.

Fourthly, passionate leaders should understand the place where God has called him or her. These leaders understand their ministry, its context and the people he or she is serving.

Four Key Principles for a Passionate Leader

1. Be Proactive: be positive. Don't wait for things to happen, make things happen. There are three types of leaders, (1)those that let things happen, (2)those that try and stop things from happening, and (3)those that make things happen. Be the type of leader that looks to God and seek Him for revelation of the future.
2. Be Reactive: always review the past game film to determine what needs to be improved for the future, what needs to be eliminated and what needs to remain.
3. Be Interactive: meet with the pastor, other team leaders and teammates for collaboration.
4. Be Committed: Vince Lombardi said that "The quality of a person's life is in direct proportion to their commitment to excellence regardless of their chosen field of endeavor."

Commitment is a part of who you are no matter what the assignment is. Your concern is to glorify God. When commitment is in the fiber of your make up, it doesn't matter what you are doing, you will be committed to it. When commitment is not a part of your make up, you won't be dedicated to anything, except that which pleases or appeals to you.

A Passionate Leader Should Develop Self-Control

In ancient times, cities were often surrounded by walls for their protection. If those walls were breached in any way, the city became vulnerable to attack from a wide variety of enemies. The maintenance of city walls, therefore, was of constant concern.

Proverbs 25:28 likens self-control to a city wall. When self-control is maintained we keep ourselves safe from forces that would wear us down, attack our weaknesses, and prey upon our failures. Scripture warns us that losing our self-control can lead to disastrous results. We may have tendencies to lose our tempers easily, gossip about neighbors and coworkers, or criticize those in authority. We may possess an unhealthy desire to own many possessions, an addiction toward food, or an obsession with television. A careless word, a broken promise, or a disrespectful action is an outward sign that our inner wall of self-control has collapsed. Weak self-control makes us vulnerable to living a life of hypocrisy, and then we lose credibility as a witness to the freedom and joy of the Christian life.

Developing self-control is not simply a matter of our willingness or a right behavior. Many have experienced the "just do it" syndrome, This is when we decide that we will finally regain control of a certain personal weakness only to find a few days later that we have succumbed once again to temptation. Self-control is not as simple as just "doing it" or "not doing it." Paul tells us that the Holy Spirit desires to guide our lives. Only He can help us overcome our sinful cravings and build self-control with staying power. As we turn ourselves over to the direction and leadership of the Holy Spirit, we will find that we are more often able to resist those things that prey upon our weaknesses. It is with the power of the Holy Spirit alone that our walls of self-control can be securely maintained.

Church Behavior and Culture is Different from any Other Organization.

What many people don't understand is that the church has a very unique culture which differs from any other organization. Simply put, the church is an organism as well as an organization.

The church's foundation should be first built on Jesus Christ. Secondly, it is developed through the pastor and the leadership's vision, purpose and core values which comes from God. This becomes the vehicle that drives the church's behavior and its culture.

The church's culture is a collection of the formal church organization, such as the pastor and officers of the church and flows down to the informal, which are the individual members. The church culture determines the type of leadership, communication, and group dynamics within the church organizational structure. Have you ever noticed when a church calls a pastor, they are trying to find someone that will match up with their culture. Most people within any organization do not want their culture upset. The members and the ministry leaders view this as the quality of church life that dictates their reason for attending that fellowship as well as what inspires and motivates them to serve their church. The end product is servanthood, which is members and guest satisfaction, along with spiritual growth, maturity and development. These essentials coalesced together will build the model or structure that the church, as an organism and organization, will operate from.

Now I have to admit, there are many who do not want to think of the church as an organization. We must, however, look at the church as an organization for the simple reason; the church has to conduct business. Within the uniqueness of the church it would help if we understood the church's behavior and its culture.

First, the churches' core values reflect the concerns a church has for its leaders, members, visitors and its surrounding community. Whether the core values are written or unwritten, these values define the manner of how the church will behave, carry out its vision and purpose which should. Core values must flow from the Great Commission and the Great Commandment.

The behavior of the church will define what type of worship, services and ministries the church will present. Behavior also defines the church's methods as well as the being and doing of the church. This leads to the business of the church, whether it is official (external) business or church (internal) business.

The pastor and the leadership will play a major role in shaping and molding the structure in accordance with the church's vision, purpose and core values. It is imperative for the leadership to examine the vision, values, history and the age of the church which makes up its personality. Believe it or not every church has a personality. Sometimes the personality is taken from the pastor. In some cases it is taken from a certain group within the church, and at times from one influential person in the church. This person is called a legitimizer. This is the person that everyone follows or takes their cue from. When this person doesn't believe in the presented concept or idea, it is likely he or she will influence others to follow them. The legitimizer is not the pastor. The personalities within the church define the roles, relationships, and behavior of the church.

Every leader should have a clear understanding of what their responsibilities are. A clearly defined set of expectations and behavior guidelines for every ministry position should be established and communicated. These expectations and guidelines may be written or oral policies within the church. Ministry leaders and their responsibilities have an influential effect on behavior, because certain members are looking for a specific type of behavior and performance of the ministry leader. Particularly the older members and mothers of the church. They prefer things done in a certain way and leaders as well as members to present themselves in a particular manner.

One thing we come to grips with is the church is built and functions around relationships. Those relationships are determined by the pastor, leaders and members. Each individual component has a specific role and responsibility within the church. Some individuals are lone rangers while other enjoy serving through relationships with others.

Each ministry responsibility will determine who the leader is required to interact with, how often, and towards what end when the church is structured properly. Now don't miss an important point when dealing with relationships, responsibilities and reactions. Everyone must be on the right bus, in the right seat, traveling in the right direction and with proper alignment for effective ministry operation. When the right people are connected with the right team and placed in ministry assignments where their passions lie, it will lead to better interactions and communication. This type of proper alignment will result in a smoother operating ministry. Think about it. When dealing with human behavior, it's difficult to like someone with whom we have no contact. We have the propensity to seek out those we like and work better with. It's common understanding that we should enjoy working with everyone in the church, yet that doesn't always happen.

People tend to work better with those they enjoy being around while doing something they take pleasure in. Ministry assignments and behaviors, that are associated only in this way, may bring about confusion and conflict when these ministry connections are disrupted. This can lead to church wars. It's like going out into the woods, finding a bee hive and sticking your arm in it. The bees are not going to rest there calmly and allow you to disrupt what they have developed over time. Church culture is the same way. We must understand any leader assigned to a ministry will encounter the established patterns of that position and group. That leader will be expected to act, lead and behave in a certain way because of the relationships developed in the past by that group. These relationships could have been developed by that leader, a prior leader or a current or former Pastor. This is how culture is developed within the church and if leaders are not careful, two different cultures are fabricated and conflict may arise. Many times this occurs simply because a certain group within the church feels their ministry or culture has been disrupted.

Let's look at it from the social system point of view. A social system is a complex set of human relationships, interacting in a variety of ways within a specific setting. Social systems within the church include all of its members, their relationships to one another, their families and the community of origin. The behavior of one member can impact, directly or indirectly, the behavior of others. Also, the social system does not have boundaries . . . it exchanges goods, ideas, culture and attitudes with the environment around it.

A church culture is the embodiment of conduct for a society that encompasses beliefs, practices, which are not always best practices, religion and understanding. It influences human behavior, even though it seldom enters into their conscious thought. Members depend upon their church culture for it gives them a sense of stability, security, understanding, the ability to respond in their manner of worship and their way of carry out business. Think about it, when the culture of the church is disturbed, things go haywire. This is why most churches fear change. They fear . . .

> their culture will become unbalanced
> their refuge will be lost
> they will not understand the new process
> they will not know how to respond to the new state of affairs or to the new way of doing business

It is essential, for pastors and leaders to be very careful when bringing about change within the church. There is a right way and a wrong way. Most of the time church leader implement change it the wrong way. I have gone about it in an improper manner on several instances. It's like someone coming to your house and telling you, that you must change the way you live in your own home. Well, you have a certain culture established in your home and you don't want anyone to upset that. It's what you and your family are accustomed to. So it is in the church. Members generally do not want things to change. It is unwise to abruptly modify the culture of any church. Change is a process and processes take time. Members want to know they will not lose what they enjoy about coming to church. For some, the church is their only source of comfort and security. All of that was stated to convey this caution, as you go about structuring or restructuring, don't do it abruptly.

First, take time to pray; seek God's leadership and guidance daily. Secondly, prioritize explaining to the membership the what, why and how. Get feedback from them and involve everyone, as much as possible, in the process. The members must have ownership of the changes. They must be assured they will not be left out. The process should be as exciting for them as it is for the pastor and leaders. Never rush the process. Remember; be anxious for nothing, but in everything through prayer and supplication. Too much change in the church at once, generates conflict or may cause members to run away. Pastors are the driving force of change and must have empathy towards their members.

Great insight is needed for pastors and leaders to enable the body to feel secure, comfortable and excited about what is to take place.

The pastor should assist the members gain understanding by allowing them to come to their own conclusions. Never try to force it. Allow time for the Holy Spirit do His work. When it is of God, He will always do His part. You've heard of a theophany right? It is when God shows up. Well, when it comes to change allow the members to have an epiphany. Allow the unexpected discerning drive of perception to bring about a rather delightful reception of change.

The Pastor and leaders should resist the urge to be pushy or overbearing in this process. Extend a welcome for the members to fill in the entire interpretation of change, and make connections of their own. When the Pastor does all the thinking for the members, there is no allowance for them to engage in the process. This usually causes the members not to invest the energy into the process which may result in them to stirring up trouble or leaving the church.

Always remember, God is not the author of confusion. He is a God of decency and order. Amen!

CHAPTER THREE

Raving Fans Not Dissatisfied Members

For many years the church has given God acceptable results. The church must always serve God with a spirit of excellence. Our service needs to be exceptional and not produce merely acceptable results. For this to take place we must all row in the same direction. If not, alignment will be off and the church will not be able to focus on or fulfill its purpose and accomplish the vision that God has set forth.

Develop a vision of excellence, centered on the needs of the members and the community. This does not mean that the church will be perfect. However, it is an image of excellence in relation to the members and community. As you look at it through the divine vision of God, what do you perceive the purpose of your church being? In other words how do you envision your church or ministry carrying out its vision futuristically?

With this in mind, the pastoral leadership team must meet and exceed expectations. The question should be asked, what the members of the church expect to receive each week they attend. Once that is determined, it must be provided consistently. It is the role of the pastor, to keep the church and the leadership team moving forward and focused upon the vision. This action reminds the team they have a responsibility to continue improving upon and exceeding expectations with flexibility. The vision will constantly adjust as the needs of the church and community transform.

In order for the pastoral leadership team to remain effective in meeting the needs of the growing congregation, they must stay abreast with what is happening around them. This will take constant effort by the team to listen to the congregants as well as evaluate the ministry's accomplishments. Vision will do one of the following in the life of church; grow it and the lack of it will cause a fall into stagnation or death.

The team must be reminded that the needs of the church will continue to change year after year. The essential components throughout the process of change are relationships and vision. Vision is in the driver seat and relationship is next to it in the passenger seat. This is why the team must assess the needs of the church and endeavor to meet those needs.

This ongoing process can only be effective when the church is properly structured. When you examine Exodus 18:13-26, you will find Jethro instructing Moses to build a team. He did this in an effort to move beyond just acceptable results to exceeding expectations. Jethro also desired them to be more effective and efficient in serving the people. As you look at the model below, think about your ministry and how it could become more proficient at producing exceptional results instead of just the acceptable.

Jethro's Model

Exodus 18:13-26

13 The next day Moses took his seat to serve as judge for the people, and they stood around him from morning till evening. 14When his father-in-law saw all that Moses was doing for the people, he said, "What is this you are doing for the people? Why do you alone sit as judge, while all these people stand around you from morning till evening?"

15Moses answered him, "Because the people come to me to seek God's will. 16Whenever they have a dispute, it is brought to me, and I decide between the parties and inform them of God's decrees and laws." 17Moses' father-in-law replied, "What you are doing is not good. 18You and these people who come to you will only wear yourselves out.

The work is too heavy for you; you cannot handle it alone. 19Listen now to me and I will give you some advice, and may God be with you. You must be the people's representative before God and bring their disputes to him. 20Teach them the decrees and laws, and show them the way to live and the duties they are to perform. 21 But select capable men from all the people—men who fear God, trustworthy men who hate dishonest gain—and appoint them as officials over thousands, hundreds, fifties and tens. 22Have them serve as judges for the people at all times, but have them bring every difficult case to you; the simple cases they can decide themselves. That will make your load lighter, because they will share it with you. 23If you do this and God so commands, you will be able to stand the strain, and all these people will go home satisfied."

Notice the last phrase, **"and all these people will go home satisfied."** *Should not this be the goal in the local church? For structure to function effectively, a team concept is imperative. Jesus had a team and their mission was to do ministry and glorify God. The text in Matthew chapter 4, beginning with verse 18 demonstrates Jesus building* His team.

18 As Jesus was walking beside the Sea of Galilee, he saw two brothers; Simon called Peter and his brother Andrew. They were casting a net into the lake, for they were fishermen. 19 "Come, follow me," Jesus said, "and I will make you fishers of men." 20 At once they left their nets and followed him. 21 Going on from there, he saw two other brothers, James son of Zebedee and his brother John. They were in a boat with their father Zebedee, preparing their nets. Jesus called them, 22 and immediately they left the boat and their father and followed him. 21 Going on from there, he saw two other brothers, James son of Zebedee and his brother John. They were in a boat with their father Zebedee, preparing their nets. Jesus called them, 22 and immediately they left the boat and their father and followed him.

Once again each person must be on the right bus, in the right seat traveling and traveling in the right direction. This will ensure those serving in ministry will have a desire to serve not with mediocre, but with exceptional results in mind.

Team members work uncompromisingly with their teammates and face incredible odds to accomplish their task, vision, purpose and or strategy. Teams thrive in an atmosphere of trust. Every member of the team must be interdependent upon one other. Team cohesiveness is a must in order to achieve set goals. Our main goal is to glorify God. God is depending on you and your church to accomplish the task He has assigned you. You must be serious about His work and the way you serve Him and His people. Once you have surrendered and committed your lives to God and the task He has called you too, there is no turning back. If one person falters, the rest of the team invests in reinforcing the breach so that the entire team bounces back together. Church leadership fails as a team and succeeds as a team. When structuring your church, carefully chose leaders to serve in positions, where their passion lies. Don't feel the need to place someone in a position in order to have a position filled.

As a team we are interdependent upon each other. It's not about popularity, but about trust and dependence. Success is realized when we think as a team and not selfishly. Never underestimate the value of fresh, innovative, and even the most abstract point of view. Diversity is good and can serve to strengthen the team. Team members adapt and learn each other's strengths and weaknesses. As leaders, we have been called to serve together as a ministry team.

Working together as a team through true fellowship will reap enormous benefits and bring about great joy.
Accountability is extremely important and necessary for every member of the team. As you think about structuring the team, there must be affirmation of the pastoral team, along with any spiritual gifts they bring to the ministry table. Celebrate fellowship within the team, as well as set goals together as you work cohesively within the church structure.

Each team member must be aware that the team is designed for cooperating not competing. Every member should have a sense of commitment to the team as well as the ministry they are involved in. In addition each person must feel comfortable to share their ideas and creativity with the team.

When you gather for meetings, be sure all participants know what type of meeting you are having. All meetings are not the same. Some are intended to deal with solving problems, while others focus on the issues at hand and answering the tough questions. Some are informational meetings. This type of meeting is intended to disseminate facts that needs to be communicated and collaborates on subject matters necessary for the effective flow of ministry. Procedural meeting types, give out essential new or updated policies, procedures or new mandates.

The following is a diagram to help you understand the effectiveness of a planned leadership team meeting.

Review   Craft   Choose   Execute

Review the ministry game plan for growth towards its vision, ensuring that it is aligned with the church's vision.

Craft the objectives and goals for the ministry team.

Choose what is best for the growth and development of the church.

And finally, **execute** *the plan with precision and passion. When precision is missing, the plan may not go smoothly.*

When passion is missing, the plan could appear to be mechanical and may not have the effectiveness to accomplish the task.

When true planning is transpiring, the purpose of the church must be center stage. We will talk more about purpose in the next chapter. When purpose is not center stage, the planning meeting could easily go in the wrong direction and cause major disaster. You plan your work and work your plan according to the ministry's purpose. When purpose is center stage, needs must be standing next to it. Whether the need is salvation, training, evangelism or a building program, the team should have its sights aimed at meeting the needs.

CHAPTER FOUR

The Significance of A Purpose Statement

It is imperative for every church to have a purpose statement to provide direction for its ministries.

A purpose statement, answers this question, "according to the Bible, what is God calling us to accomplish?" A purpose statement is vision-driven and dictates direction. It quantifies the importance of knowing God's vision for your church. It is a brief, biblical statement of what the church is to enthusiastically be doing!

A purpose statement is the umbrella over all the church's ministry activities. All goals and activities a church is involved in should fit comfortably under the overarching ministry and purpose of the church. When a goal or activity does not fit underneath the purpose, either the purpose is not broad enough or the activity or goal is not within the purpose's range. When goals or activities do not fit under the purpose, it may be an indication it is time to re-evaluate and re-group.

A purpose statement is succinct and simple. It is generally short and concise. The size or length of a purpose statement makes the determination whether it is brief or not. How short is brief? A good purpose statement is a short, single, well-written sentence. The purpose statement should be in a summarized format, simply stating what the church or ministry should be doing in a clear-cut, defined method. The purpose statement will have a biblical flavor to it, ensuring divine guidance by the Word of God. It must never disagree with the teachings of Scripture. A biblical purpose is from God. He may reveal your purpose through the Bible or maybe through another method or medium. It is God alone who reveals to the church its purpose.

Each ministry should convey its purpose in statement form so members can be aware of and understand it's overall aspiration. A purpose statement may be conveyed in verbal and written forms. When people encounter the written purpose statement, they are intellectually aware of where the ministry is headed. Writing the statement out presses one to collect their thoughts and process them thoroughly with clarity. Placing the purpose statement in written form puts it in a medium, which can be communicated in a variety of ways. It may be placed strikingly on a standing board within the main entry way, on the church's brochure, weekly bulletin or in a quarterly newsletter. In these varied mediums the statement is visible and serves as a regular reminder.

The purpose statement can also be read and discussed in your New Members class. In addition, it can be framed or placed on a wall plaque and hung in the foyer of the church's meeting area. Another interesting variation to its distribution method may be to place it on wallet-sized cards for leadership to use when on visitation or witnessing to the lost or un-churched.

A final defining element of significance for the purpose statement is that it highlights what the church is to carry out. It is your church's principal goal or task. It is not what you want to accomplish, but what God wants to do through you. What does God want your church to achieve? Do Scriptures directly or indirectly answer this question? How are you to minister to the people you are to reach, teach and nurture? Matthew 20:19-20 speaks directly to it. Are you pursuing, winning and assisting in the spiritual development of the lost in accordance with this passage? Are you helping others to grow closer to Christ and experience the fullness of the Christian life? There are several additional questions that may assist you in evaluating what your ministry should be engaged in to expand the kingdom of God.

The first question that should be asked is "what is God revealing to us that needs to be carried out?" Christ has commissioned the church to reach the lost and make disciples.

The next question encourages leaders to envision the church's future without a biblical purpose. Where would we be if we continued on this present journey, without a biblical purpose for another two to five years?

A follow-up question centers on leadership. Are the key leaders aware of where the ministry is presently and what its future is? Are the leaders in alignment and agreement with this direction? The final question is whether the leadership willing to do what it takes to navigate the ministry in a new direction through the power of the Holy Spirit?

A purpose statement uniquely defines the role of a particular church or ministry. Remember, the purpose statement reflects the biblical mandate as a part of the church's vision, core values, and ministry context. It helps people to move in the same direction. In a simple yet profound way, the purpose statement should capture the reason the church or the ministry exists. As the foundational vision of the church is better developed, the purpose statement will change. As the church becomes more effective and efficient in carrying out their purpose, the purpose statement may change. In addition, as the church finds new and innovative ways to serve the community, the purpose statement may change again.

Don't be tempted to look at other ministry purpose statements and adopt one of them. They may not fit the vision that God has given to your church. Never rely on another's purpose statement for your ministry. Always seek the leadership of the Holy Spirit in developing your own purpose statement. The purpose statement is essential for ministry budgeting and calendar planning for the church.

A contrast of vision and purpose
Vision and purpose are similar and different.

Purpose	*Vision*
Purpose defines	Vision is a snapshot
Purpose is used in planning	Vision communicates
Purpose is shorter	Vision is longer
Purpose informs	Vision inspires
Purpose is doing	Vision is seeing
Purpose is from the mind	Vision is from the heart
Purpose clarifies	Vision challenges

Developing Your Purpose Statement

Answering the following questions can facilitate your purpose statement.

➤ What should we be doing, according to the Bible?
➤ Is the purpose statement understandable? Is the purpose statement clear?
➤ Is the purpose statement unique and specific to what God is calling us to accomplish? Is it captivating?

Activity

1. Think about appropriate scriptures concerning the purpose of the church.
2. Identify key words or ideas that describe what makes your church unique.
3. Develop short, essential phrases to describe your church.

Drafting a Preliminary Purpose Statement for Your Church

1. Within your leadership team, begin to work on and develop a purpose statement.
2. Pondering over the following steps may facilitate the process:

   ➤ Identify appropriate scriptures relating to the purpose of your church or ministry.
   ➤ Circle key words or phrases in these verses that describe what makes your church unique.
   ➤ Develop short essential phrases that may describe your church or ministry.
   ➤ Draft a preliminary purpose statement for your church.

Evaluation of Your Purpose Statement:

   ➤ Does it identify your primary focus group?
   ➤ Does it clarify the needs you feel lead to meet?
   ➤ Does it identify three to five essential ministry areas?
   ➤ Is it accurate, enduring, concise, memorable, and energizing?

Things to Ponder:

   ➤ Does your purpose statement focus on strengths?
   ➤ Does it respond to challenges and needs?
   ➤ Does it reflect the vision and core values?
   ➤ Does it inspire involvement and commitment?
   ➤ Does it reflect the unique plan and purpose of God for your church?

Five principles to remember!

1. Is it meant for our church to do?
2. Is it time for your church to do it?
3. Is it going to edify the body?
4. Is it going to evangelize the unsaved?
5. Is it going to exalt the savior?
6. Will it elevate the saints?

Now write out a sample purpose statement

CHAPTER FIVE

Plan Your Work and Work Your Plan
According to Purpose

Developing a ministry strategy plan is essential for the structure of your church.

A well organized leader asks themselves at the start of each day of ministry these questions:

➤ What is it that I want to accomplish today to advance the kingdom of God, in light of the purpose of the church and the task before me?
➤ What do I need to accomplish to ensure these things are done? What are the resources needed to accomplish the task?
➤ Whose approval is needed?
➤ How will I know the task is completed?

If these questions are not asked or answered with intention, it may indicate that you need to begin planning. Planning and time management are the mainstream ingredients for good stewardship.

If you do not effectively plan, you may find yourself carried along with the demands, which occur along the way. Without planning, at the end of the day you may find you have accomplished only pieces of your tasks. Poor planning leaves the church with a sense of stagnation. Proper plans and effective execution facilitate a strong sense of accomplishment. As ministry leaders, we have a stewardship responsibility to God. We must ensure that we manage our time wisely. Therefore, it is best that you plan effectively.

This chapter is designed to guide you through a step by step outline for planning your day to day activities. Planning is the process necessary for the accomplishment of a task or an assignment.

Activity

A Step By Step Process for Planning

The Outline

- ➤ Write out a ministry purpose statement for your ministry.
- ➤ Establish your objectives around your purpose statement.
- ➤ Assess your needs and resources.
- ➤ Establish your goals around your objectives.
- ➤ Create a list of alternative actions to reach your objectives.
- ➤ Think through the consequences of each alternative action.

This ministry purpose statement will integrate with the church's overall purpose statement. It is the main guide used for determining the objectives for the church ministry tasks as assigned to your specific ministry. This statement usually includes elements, which meet spiritual, social, emotional, and physical needs of the people your ministry serves.

As previously examined in the section on purpose, ministry purpose statements are to be brief yet comprehensive. This purpose statement outlines its objectives, such as:

- ➤ To reach and disciple people for Christ.
- ➤ To minister to families and singles
- ➤ To have a balanced worship experience.

A ministry purpose statement include input from all groups involved in carrying out the ministry task.

Activity

Take some time, with your ministry team, to write a ministry purpose statement draft. Consider taking this draft and sharing it with your pastor and leadership team.

PURPOSE STATEMENT DRAFT

First Try:

_____

_____

_____

_____

_____

Revised Edition:

_____

_____

_____

_____

_____

Draft to Present to Groups

_____

_____

_____

_____

_____

List those persons you need to meet with to discuss the purpose statement:

_____

_____

_____

_____

_____

_____

What are your plans to discuss this purpose statement with the necessary persons and obtain the needed approvals?

_____

_____

_____

_____

_____

Establish Your Objectives Around Your Purpose Statement.

An objective is a future desired state or outcome. Remember objectives only have meaning for the setting in which they are developed. For every event planned, there must be a clearly defined objective. An example would be the person who serves as a Youth Director would need an objective defined for each youth event planned (youth revival, youth rally, etc.) Objectives may differ for each specialized event.

When you examine the defined objectives, ask the following questions:

1. Is this objective essential to the accomplishment of the ministry purpose statement?
2. Are there any individuals or groups that can accomplish this objective better than the ministry I serve in can?
3. Are there other individuals or group already doing this project?
4. Are there resources, equipment, staff, volunteers, and/or finances available to address this objective with a reasonable assurance the objective will be accomplished?

Make an Assessment of Your Needs and Resources.

Several questions need to be addressed when assessing your needs and resources:

- ➤ What equipment and resources do I currently possess?
- ➤ What staff (salaried or volunteer) are assessable to the ministry?
- ➤ What finances are available to the ministry for programs/events?
- ➤ What prayer and spiritual support is available?

Activity

Stop! Think about your current ministry situation. Review your ministry calendar, in light of the purpose statement you drafted. Write an objective for each planned event.

Remember . . . prioritized planning will save your ministry time and energy in the end.

Establish Your Goals Around Your Objectives, Needs and Resources.

Now we are ready to prepare a goal for each objective. Goals are the succession of steps which identify the specific actions necessary to move toward the accomplishment of the objective. A goal says what has to be done. It also includes a deadline or a specific time when the task will be completed. Goals answer the question . . . what is to happen and within what time period. Goals must be attainable. This will allow you to evaluate your efforts at various intervals throughout the event journey. In other words, goals clarify what is going to happen and when. They will assist you in knowing whether you are winning or losing.

Activity

Review your objectives and prepare goals for each objective. Make sure your goals are tailored for your particular situation. Remember that goals must include a measurable event that will be accomplished within a specified time. A well-written goal will include information needed to measure when it is achieved and the quality of your stewardship. Ask these questions when identifying your goals:

➤ Does the goal identify something specifically to be accomplished?
➤ Does the goal include a way to measure the achievement of the goal?
➤ Does the goal establish an assessment time to determine whether it has been accomplished?

Create a List of Alternative Actions to Reach Your Objectives

_____

_____

_____

_____

_____

Preparing Action Plans

For each goal set, completion of one or more Action Plan Sheets is necessary. These sheets will guide and assist in monitoring your work day by day. Action plans should include specific assignments, responsibility and accountability. The focus of these sheets will be the actions, needed for the goal to be attained. Action plans also assist the staff, volunteer team and or committee supervisor by keeping everyone on track.

The preparation of these action plan sheets assists the ministry to stay on target with deadlines set thereby facilitating the meeting of established goals. When you remain on track with your objectives, you will have greater assurance of accomplishing your goal as detailed in your objective.

If your ministry is not meeting set goals, you will then have the task of discovering why. It may be that the goals need revision or have proven themselves unrealistic in light of available resources or some other limitation. Another possibility is your team has become distracted from focusing on your goals. Whatever reasons you discover, you must determine where you are and where you are headed.

Implementation of the Action Plan

It is now time to act on what you have planned. Your team may find it helpful, during the implementation process, to keep track of all the goals and action plans on a time line. This means you take the goals and action plans from your calendar and chart them out.

With your time line chart completed, you are enabled to focus on the objective you have developed. The time line will correlate with the goals and action plans to accomplish the objective. When you use a time line, it will facilitate you planning your work for the month. Once the action item is completed, the timeline makes it easy to measure your project. This vital tool will also facilitate meetings and keep everyone abreast of deadlines in a timely fashion.

Evaluation of Time

Objectives are assessed by how well goals are met. Using the time line, you can assess quickly whether each goal has been met. Celebrate your accomplishments. Always keep in mind that small gains are progressively moving your ministry towards the accomplishments of your objectives. Give yourself a "that-a-boy or that-a-girl" and share it with your team members. If you are unsuccessful in meeting any of your goals, you must determine why. The team will most likely need to review the game film to conclude the reason the goals were not met. The following questions may facilitate in the discovery of the goals not being met:

- ➤ Was it an unrealistic goal? If so adjust or revise it for the next time.
- ➤ Was the goal unattained because of distractions? If so, decide what can be done to avoid this next time. Make definitive detailed resolutions.
- ➤ Was the goal unattained due to lack of staff resources or poor staff performance? If so, you may consider assignment sheets with clear and precise duties outlined. Training may be another consideration to offset poor performance, detailing a comprehensive resolution.
- ➤ Was the goal not realized due to a new limitation imposed? If so, do you have the authority to change it. Outline another approach for the next time.
- ➤ Did a change take place in the community, which made the goal not worth pursuing? If so, decide whether to continue it.

Your evaluation will be an effective measurement of how you moved towards accomplishing your objectives. It also serves as a tool to provide comments as well as building block towards your next years' planning.

SUMMARY

God's called leaders are responsible to be good stewards of our time, talents and resources.
God made a plan for us . . . can we do any less for Him? Be encouraged to give God your very best!

PLAN YOUR WORK AND WORK YOUR PLAN!

CHAPTER SIX

Church Structure

Questions we need to ask:

What structure will accomplish our <u>purpose</u>, to carry out God's vision for our church?

How do we <u>move</u> from where we are to where we are called to go?

What must <u>change</u>?

What must <u>remain</u> the same?

This is where you replay the game film of the church. Reflect on the past. What worked and what did not?

Using your spiritual imagination, and the filter of prayer and communion with God, how do you see your church in the future? What <u>would be</u> the <u>most effective</u> way to minister <u>to the people</u> of your community as well as those attending your church?

The pastor and the leadership team must ask the question, how will we facilitate getting this ministry to where God wants us to be?

Jesus states in John 5:19-20, "I assure you: the Son is not able to do anything on His own, but only what He sees the Father doing. For whatever the Father does, the Son also does these things in the same way. For the Father loves the Son and shows Him everything He is doing, and He will show Him greater works than these so that you will be amazed."

Additional questions that should be asked of the leadership team: How do we advance the kingdom of God according to the Great Commission and the Great Commandment? How do we to help the church find it purpose or re-establish its purpose?

Pastors and nominating teams must place called leaders in position who have been gifted by God with a passion to serve. Leader must know why they are called to serve within their respective ministry. The church has the responsibility to provide training and communicate what the expectations of the church are. Pastors must assist leaders as well as empower them to do ministry.

One way for the church to be successful in structuring ministries and carrying out the Great Commission is to operate out of the five functions of the church. The first New Testament church fulfilled these five functions in accordance with Acts 2:41-47.

The book of Acts teaches us the New Testament church has five functions, plus stewardship. When the church operates out of these functions, it generates the momentum and the motivation to fulfill the Great Commission. If the church is to be effective in carrying out the mandate of Christ these functions are essential.

The five functions of the church are:

> *Evangelism* is the process of sharing the Gospel with a lost and dying, world winning them to Christ thereby enabling them to enter the kingdom of God.
> *Discipleship* is the process of building kingdom leaders equipping believers to serve by engaging people in actions that move them toward spiritual transformation.
> *Fellowship* creates opportunities for persons to experience camaraderie with other believers. These experiences promote encouragement and the building of a sense of community within the church family.
> *Ministry* exists to build up the body of Christ to accomplish the work of service within the church.
> *Worship* is the experience of celebrating God's grace and mercy, the proclamation of God's truth, and the evangelization the lost.
> *Stewardship* is the process of maintaining, managing and educating the church on the importance of being a good steward for God.

CONTEMPOARY MINISTRY STRUCTURE BREAKDOWN

Ministry Directors are responsible for planning, implementing and overseeing each ministry area that falls within that particular ministry function area.

Ministry Coordinators work harmoniously with the Ministry Director and other persons involved. Each coordinator will only operate within their assigned ministry.

Sample Ministry Position Descriptions

Ministry Directors: *Each Ministry Director will be responsible for ensuring that all components of the ministry teams are functioning properly. As minor ministry issues develop, seek to resolve them. Major issues that occur are referred to the attention of the pastor for resolution. These issue types may be addressed by the*

Executive Leadership Team: *The ministry director works closely with each team leader of their respective ministry, varied communication of those items necessary for effective ministry productivity and purpose of the church to advance the kingdom of God. Responsible for meeting with their Ministry Team Leaders at least once a month,* Ministry Directors are expected to report of their respective ministry during the designated meeting with the pastor. This ensures the pastor is always kept abreast of the state and concerns of each ministry within the church.

Ministry Director

The Ministry Director will be responsible for assimilating people in the church, based on their spiritual gifts, personalities and interests. This involves assisting with teaching the new members orientation courses lead in administering the Spiritual Gifts inventories. These courses and assessments help members identify and understand their gifts, how they can be used in ministry and advises members of opportunities within the church and related ministries.

Ministry Area/Department	Ministry
Position	Ministry director
Accountable To	Pastor
Ministry Target	Church
Position Status	Volunteer
Position May Be Filled By	Church member
Minimum Maturity Level	Stable, mature Christian
Spiritual Gifts	Exhortation • Pastor/shepherd • Administration • Teaching
Talents or Abilities Desired	Able to coordinate and harmonize a group of people
Best Personality Traits	Dependable • Cooperative • leadership
Passion For	Involving all Christians in the work of the ministry according to their individual spiritual gifts, personalities and interests
Length of Service Commitment	One to three years minimum

Anticipated Time Commitments

1. Doing ministry/preparing for ministry: three hours each week
2. Participating in meetings/training: one hour each week as needed

Responsibilities/Duties

1. Collaborate with other ministry leaders for enlistment and placement of individuals in ministry positions
2. Become familiar with the ministry opportunities within and associated within the church and maintain an updated list of available positions and tasks
3. Teach the new member's orientation course as needed for new believers, new Christians, and current members. Train others to teach the New Members Orientation courses
4. Administer the Spiritual Gifts inventory to all church members interested in serving within ministry positions, especially new members
5. Interview members who complete the new member's orientation to assist them find their place to serve in the church based on their spiritual gifts, personalities and interests

6. Maintain a record of who is serving in each position
7. Assist, develop and maintain updated ministry descriptions for every ministry opportunity in the church
8. In addition, oversee and manage the following ministries;
   - New Members Orientation Ministry
   - Men's Ministry
   - Women's Ministry
   - Youth Ministry
   - Children's Ministry
   - Single's Ministry
   - Missions
   - Prison's Ministry
   - New Member's Assimilation ☐
   - Prayer Ministry

Discipleship Ministry Director

The Discipleship Ministry Director is responsible for planning, implementing and overseeing the Sunday School, Bible Study programs and specialize training of the church.

Ministry Area/Department	General staff/administration
Position	Discipleship ministry director
Accountable To	Pastor
Ministry Target	Sunday School & Bible Study
Position Status	Volunteer
Position May Be Filled By	Church member
Minimum Maturity Level	Stable, maturing Christian
Spiritual Gifts	Administration • Exhortation • Teaching
Talents or Abilities Desired	Practical organizational and planning skills • Effective Communicator Dependable • Leader
Best Personality Traits	Equipping the saints for ministry • Seeing people grow
Passion For	through studying God's Word
Length of Service Commitment	One year to three years.

Anticipated Time Commitments

1. Doing ministry/preparing for ministry: four hours each week
2. Participating in meetings/training: one hour minimum each month

Responsibilities/Duties

1. Plan and implement the Sunday School and Bible Study ministries
2. Establish curriculum
3. Order curriculum and supplies needed for teaching
4. Recruit teachers.
5. Plan and conduct meetings, seminars and activities to train teachers
6. Schedule special seminars or classes for specific group needs (divorce care, parenting, finances, marriage enrichment, etc)
7. Manage budget for Discipleship Ministry function area

Evangelism Ministry Director

The Evangelism Ministry Director is responsible for overseeing and implementing the church evangelism program, training volunteers and actively participating in the evangelism ministry to influence others for Christ and bring them into the church.

Ministry Area/Department	Ministry
Position	Evangelism Ministry Director
Accountable To	Pastor
Ministry Target	Visitors, unsaved and un-churched.
Position Status	Volunteer
Position May Be Filled By	Church member
Minimum Maturity Level	Stable, maturing Christian
Spiritual Gifts	Administration • Evangelism
Talents or Abilities Desired	Proficient organizational skills
	Excellent leadership skills
Best Personality Traits Passion For	Leading people to Christ • Helping others in their spiritual growth
Length of Service Commitment	*One to three year minimum*

Anticipated Time Commitments

1. Doing ministry/preparing for ministry: two hours each week
2. Participating in meetings/training: one hour each month

Responsibilities/Duties

1. Follow up with visitors and prospects that have completed forms requesting prayer, asking questions about the ministry, indicating curiosity about salvation, etc

2. Work with Evangelism Team to organize and assign visits to prospects
3. Serve as an encourager/counselor for those who come forward for salvation during or following church services
4. Pray regularly for the evangelism ministry, for those who will be visited and for specific names of people needing salvation
5. Be able to share your faith with others, using life experiences through Christ and salvation testimony as well as Scripture
6. Be familiar with Scriptures that explain how to become a Christian and provide assurance of salvation
7. Provide training to those who become involved in the Evangelism Ministry
    a. Provide ongoing support and training materials as needed.
    b. Plan a course or seminar at least yearly, for training and reinforcement of evangelism methods and church's evangelism program. Teach what to do and what not to do. Explore new opportunities, etc
8. Plan evangelistic event and follow-up related to small groups
9. Assist evangelism event coordinator with planning and follow-up

Fellowship Ministry Director

The Fellowship Ministry Director is responsible for planning, implementing and overseeing the fellowship and event planning functions of the church.

Ministry Area/Department	Ministry
Position	Fellowship Ministry Director
Accountable To	Pastor
Ministry Target	Fellowship and event planning
Position Status	Volunteer
Position May Be Filled By	Church member
Minimum Maturity Level	Stable, maturing Christian
Spiritual Gifts	Administration • Exhortation
Talents or Abilities Desired	Good organizational and planning skills
	• Good communicator
Best Personality Traits	Dependable • Leader
Passion For	Encouraging, and building relationships
Length of Service Commitment	One year to three years.

Anticipated Time Commitments

1. Doing ministry/preparing for ministry: four hours each week
2. Participating in meetings/training: one hour minimum each month

Responsibilities/Duties

1. Oversee organize and manage fellowship events. Events would include Sunday morning refreshments, picnics, family gatherings, Church Anniversary, Fall Festival Family and Friends' day and other church events
2. Recruit volunteers or contact appropriate ministry directors to assist with food preparation/ service, set up facilities, decorations, equipment needs, publicity, etc
3. Manage budget for Fellowship Ministry function area

Note: All enlisted persons must be approved by the Pastor.

Worship Ministry Director

The worship Ministry Director will oversee the weekly celebrative, meaningful worship services within the church. He/she will also direct the church's music ministries as well as to those involved in the worship ministry.

Ministry Area/Department	Ministry
Position	Worship Ministry Director
Accountable To	Pastor
Ministry Target	Church
Position Status	Volunteer
Position May Be Filled By	Church member
Minimum Maturity Level	Stable, mature Christian
Spiritual Gifts	Exhortation
Talents or Abilities Desired	Experience and/or education in the music field
Best Personality Traits	• Able to lead and promote unity within a group
	Outgoing • Energetic
Passion For	Glorifying God and edifying the saints through music and worship
Length of Service Commitment	One to three years.

Anticipated Time Commitments

1. Doing ministry/preparing for ministry: four hours each week
2. Participating in meetings/training: one hour each week

Responsibilities/Duties

1. Oversee the planning of a celebrative and meaningful worship services in conjunction with the Pastor and Music Ministry Coordinator.
2. Ensure pray-ers are scheduled for the worship service, in conjunction with the Prayer Coordinator
3. Ensure that the media ministry is staffed and ready for worship service and other events the church has scheduled
4. Ensure proper maintenance of musical instruments
5. Make sure platform/sanctuary is properly arranged for the weekly services and special productions
6. Ensure that offering is carried out in accordance with establish protocols
7. Pray for, uplift and minister to those who are involved in the worship ministry

Stewardship Ministry Director

The Stewardship Ministry Director is responsible for overseeing and managing the finances of the church.

Ministry Area/Department	Finance
Position	Stewardship Ministry Director
Accountable To	Pastor
Ministry Target	Finance
Position Status	Volunteer
Position May Be Filled By	Church member
Minimum Maturity Level	Stable, maturing Christian
Spiritual Gifts	Administration • Accounting • Teaching Good with figures • Discreet • Excellent organizational skills
Talents or Abilities Desired	Good organizational and planning skills • Good communicator
Best Personality Traits	Dependable • Leader
Passion For	Equipping the saints in being good stewards for God •
Length of Service Commitment	One year to three years.

Anticipated Time Commitments

1. Doing ministry/preparing for ministry: six hours each week
2. Participating in meetings/training: one hour each month or as needed

Responsibilities/Duties

1. Oversee and manage the finances of the church
2. Implement a stewardship emphasis' plan for the church.
3. Manage and maintain a competent finance counting team
4. Seeks ways to invest the monetary of the church
5. Reconcile all accounts for the church, compose and communicate regular reports to the Operations Manager and Pastor
6. Make necessary deposits for the church after each offering opportunity
7. Attend to other financial matters regularly within the church
8. Maintain accurate records of member contributions and prepare year-end statements for each member
9. In accordance with policies and procedures
10. Maintain accurate records of all church income and prepare comparative reports to annual budget projections
11. Maintain accurate records of all church expenditures and compare to budget projections

12. Prepare and communicate comprehensive reports to the pastor if expenditures exceed budget allowances
13. Prepare recurring financial reports for the Operations Manager and the Pastor
14. Prepare checks endorsements for monthly church expenses and obligations
15. Prepare checks for contributions to missions work and other special endeavors
16. Prepare reimbursement checks for staff/volunteerism accordance with established protocols

Utilize these as samples, for instructional purposes only. Your church under the direction of the Holy Spirit will need to develop job descriptions for the specific ministries of your church.

From my experience and estimation, following a structure is essential for the church to have a process to follow.

These processes have been adapted from resources and studies I have presented and found to be effective to assist the church to understand whether they are winning or losing, progressing or standing still. The following is a more traditional model verse the above contemporary model.

TRADITIONAL MINISTRY STRUCTURE BREAKDOWN

Executive Leadership Team

- Serve as a bridge between the church membership and the ministries/committees of the church

- Executive Leadership Planning Team facilitate the church body in carrying out its vision, purpose and core values

- Coordinate the church's calendar and activities

- Provide monthly ministry updates to ministries regarding their respective ministries.

- Compiles/submits annual budgets for assigned ministries/committees and makes recommendations to the church

Detailed below is the layout of the Executive Leadership Team. Your team may and can look different, depending upon the ministries and ministry leaders within your church. It is essential for the Executive Leadership Team to pray and seek God for His direction, leadership and wisdom. When you follow His leadership, you will be led in prosperous paths.

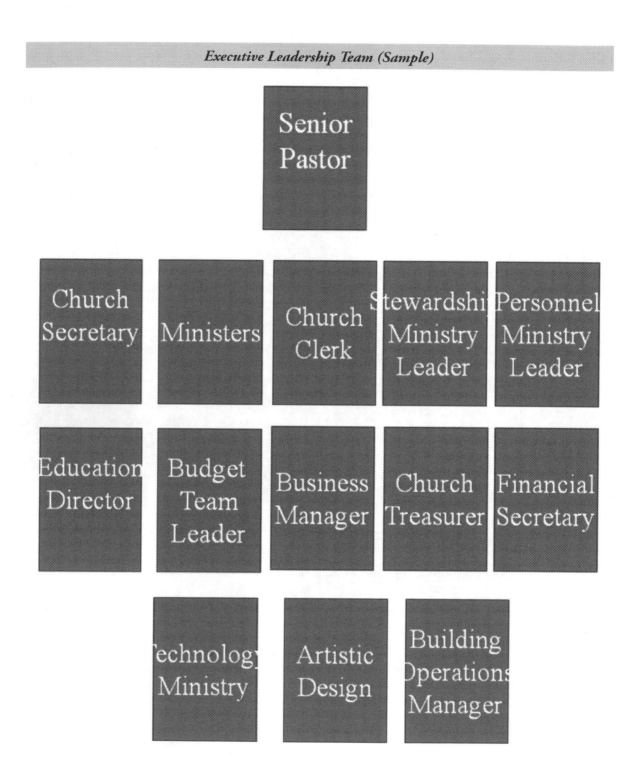

Deacons & Deaconess Ministry

Deacons Ministry

- Lead in the Family Group Ministr/Serve as an extension of the Pastor

- Work together, in partnership with the Pastor, to carry out the ministries of the Church

1. In collaboration with the Pastor, recruit and train servant leaders.
2. Make monthly visits with those families that have been assigned to him/her.
3. Make hospital and sick visits with persons of assigned family group.
4. Assist new members to become assimilated within the new church family.
5. Serve as a communication conduit for his/her Ministry area.
6. Serve as visible godly example, to the congregation of a mature disciple of Christ living a Spirit-filled life devoted to God.
7. Focus on specific needs of his /her assigned families within the church.
8. Visit a minimum of five homes each month or as needed.
9. Meet with the entire family group once each quarter or as needed to communicate information.
10. Plan and complete at least one group outing once a year.
11. Servant leaders will collaborate with the Pastor to communicate any situation that warrants his attention.

Deaconess Ministry

1. Responsible for preparation of Holy Communion each month
2. Work in partnership with the appropriate Deacon within the Family Group Ministry and other responsibilities as needed
3. Support any ministry or service effort as needed and directed by the Pastor

Trustee Ministry

1. Responsible for protection and conservation of the building maintenance and equipment of the Church
2. Work in partnership with the Building Operations Manager to ensure that every aspect of the Church's property is well kept and maintained
3. Responsible for the oversight of the building and property
4. Responsible for the security of the building on a rotating basis
5. Act as a representative of church and in the community

Fellowship Ministry

1. Coordinate various events for the church with the Church Secretary and/or person wanting to host the event
2. Coordinate with the needed Church ministry leaders, where appropriate, for events occurring on Church property
3. Coordinate with the Encouragers Ministry Leader as needed
4. Coordinate with the Usher Ministry Leader as needed

Fellowship Ministry (sample)

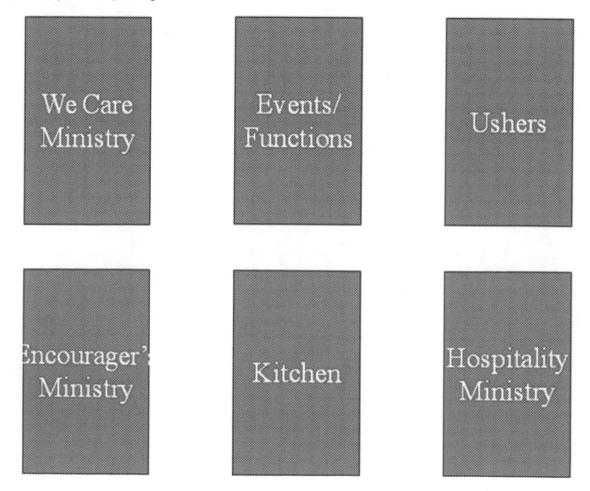

Missions Ministry

1. Inspire the members of the church to support missions both locally and internationally
2. Provide age and gender appropriate Missions Circles to further learn about mission opportunities and needs
3. Support the Convention objectives

Women's Ministry

1. Reach, introduce and win women into a growing relationship with God through Jesus Christ at this local church and its surrounding communities
2. Develop women of all ages into mature and contributing Kingdom citizens
3. Influence women in such a way that they become effective servants for Christ in their homes, work places and at this local church
4. Meet the unique fellowship needs of women through Scripture-focused opportunities
5. Develop women relationally that we may accurately reflect Christ in the world and win others to Him through lifestyle witnessing

Men's Ministry

1. The Men's Ministry is designed to create a well-balanced, meaningful ministry that reaches and involves all men of the church. It consists of three main areas:
2. Outreach/Evangelism
3. Spiritual Development
4. Missions/Ministry Involvement

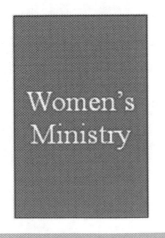

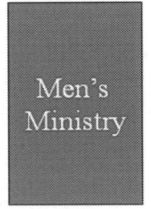

Youth Ministry

1. Provide spiritual, educational and cultural opportunities that support the overall mission of the church

2. Inspire youth towards a committed, Christ-centered life through partnership with church organizations
3. Provide educational and spiritual tools to the youth of Watts Chapel and the surrounding community

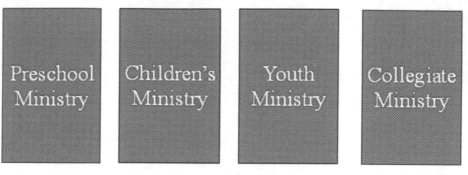

Media Ministry

1. Responsible for the efficient operations of the church's media equipment, including not limited to, the sound system, duplication system, and/or special lighting
2. Participate in any and all training as it relates to church media equipment and ministry protocols
3. Committed to be dependable and timely when scheduled for church events; when unable to be present, technician is responsible for securing a replacement
4. Assist, develop and implement a maintenance program all media equipment
5. Recommend any appropriate upgrades and/or changes to the media equipment and or ministry protocol
6. Provide input regarding the Media Ministry annual budget

Creative Arts Ministry

1. Responsible for developing and implementing the Creative Arts Ministry within the church
2. Coordinate the Drama Ministry, Praise Dancers, Christian Steppers and Mime teams
3. Provide training and participate in training as needed
4. Coordinate events that occur both within the church and in the community
5. Communicate with the various Creative Arts Ministry Team leaders as needed

Music Ministry

1. Responsible for planning the music presentation for the various choirs/ ensembles
2. Responsible for coordinating all choir ensembles events within the church
3. Responsible for coordinating all choir ensembles events outside of the church
4. Responsible for communicating all needed items with the various choirs ensembles and/or musicians
5. Be willing to participate in music training and worship as needed
6. Be willing to provide training to the Music Ministry Team as needed

Finance Ministry Team

1. Be committed to understanding and practicing biblical stewardship including growth in giving through the local church
2. Possess a genuine concern for the church and fulfillment of its mission
3. Participate in ongoing training and carry out assigned responsibilities

Participate in all Finance Ministry Team meetings as needed

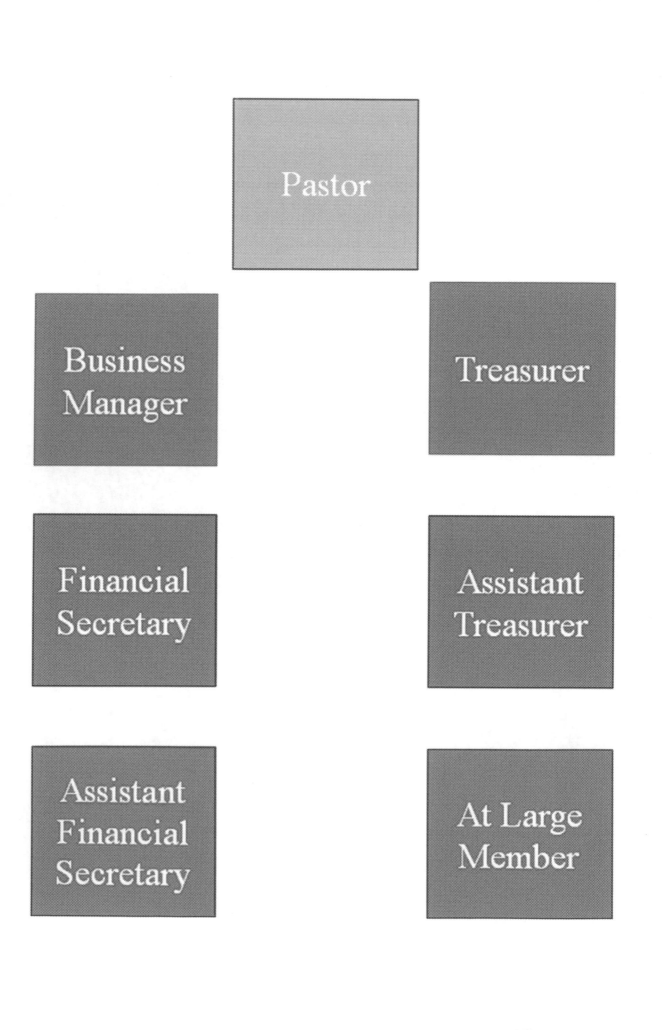

Personnel Ministry

1. Responsible for establishing and facilitating personnel policies
2. Responsible for communicating with the Pastor regarding any personnel issues
3. Responsible for communicating with the appropriate personnel any issues that arise

Education Ministry

1. Responsible for coordinating Educational program as directed by the Pastor
2. Responsible for coordinating and developing the weekly Bible Studies
3. Responsible for working with the various ministry leaders regarding needed educational programs

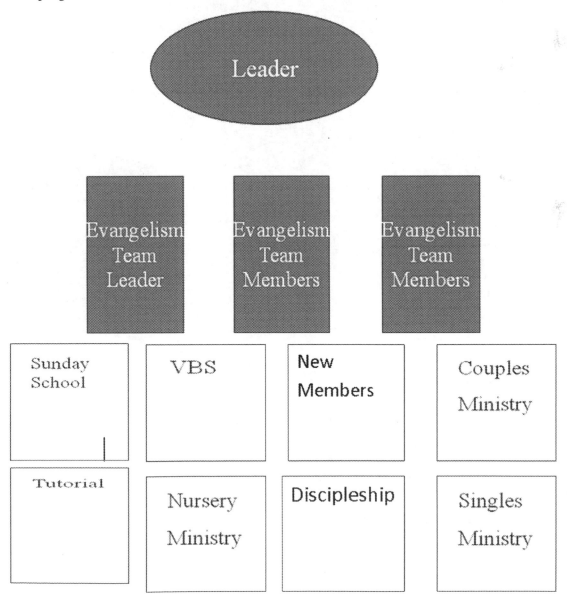

Evangelism Ministry

1. Responsible for the outreach of the surrounding community
2. Responsible for coordinating with the Sunday School Superintendent regarding follow up with Sunday School visitors
4. Responsible for coordinating the follow up of Church visitors

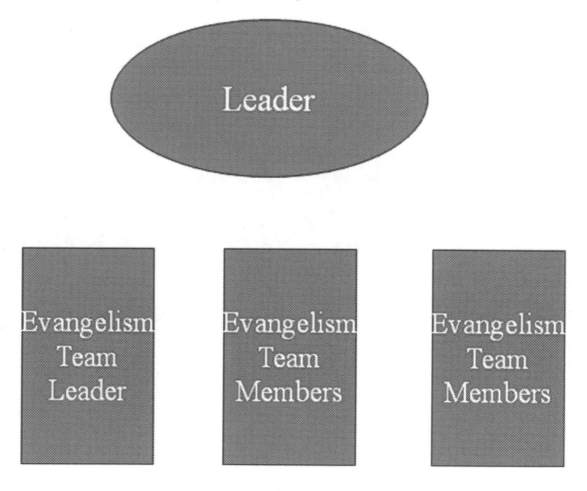

Ministry Liaisons

1. Responsible for ensuring that all components of their team ministries are functioning properly
2. Work closely with the various team leaders of their respective ministries and communicate any items necessary for effective productivity
3. Seek to resolve any minor issues as needed
4. Discuss any major issues with the Deacon Ministry representative to the Executive Leadership Planning Team

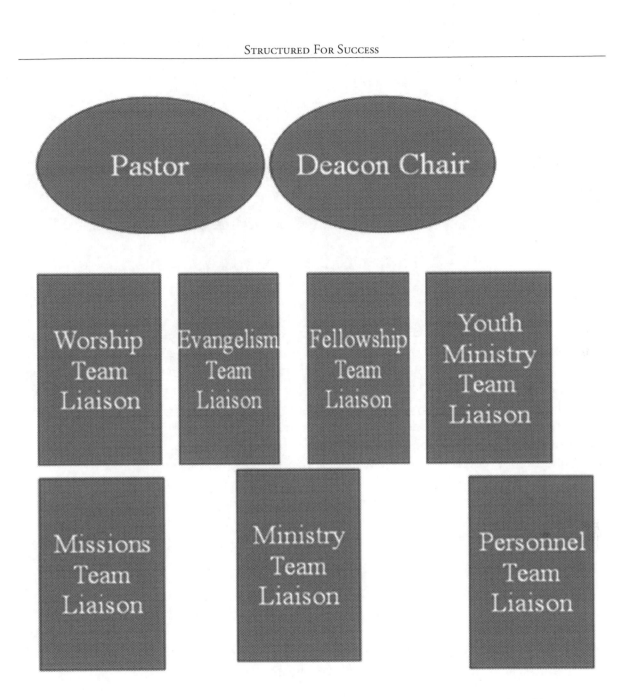

Remember your team may look different. You can structure it according to your church's ministries and the leadership of your church.

CHAPTER SEVEN

Your Churches' Process

What is process? Process is movement along with procedures to help the church get from point A to point B. When a church does not know how to get from A to B, then the possibility increases that they will not be productive with the ministries of the church. Let's use sports as an example. Take baseball. Baseball has a process. Each player must understand the process or they can cause their team to lose the game. When the player gets up to bat, he has to be cognitive of which way to run upon hitting the ball. If not, he may run in the wrong direction. The batter may run to third base instead of to first, causes the team an out. There are many members within the local church running in the wrong direction. A process is needed to help them understand which way to run.

Remember, write the vision, make it plan and run with it. The following is only an example of a "process" I used for a fellowship I pastored. It will illustrate for you how to formulate your own process. Every church's process will be different, according to the church's vision, purpose and values.

Process: Join Christ >>> Grow in Christ>>> Serve Christ>> Reach People for Christ

How do the weekly programs fit into the process?

Sunday Worship>>> (Proclamation of God's Word) Sunday School >>> (Education of the saints) Bible Study >>>(Edification of the saints)

How does your church illustrate the process?

Through effective communication and the New Members Orientation.

How does your church measure each stage of the process?

Through evaluating the numbers, and how members move through the process.

How does your church move members through the process?

Through Worship, Sunday School, Bible Study and New Members Orientation.

How does your church position its members to experience God's transforming power?

Through biblical preaching and teaching.

The process of your church is designed to partner with God;

Through prayer and Bible Study.

What happens when a person join the Body of Christ at your church?

When new members join, they are taken to the new member's area to complete the new member's profile. Three copies are made. One copy is given to the church office for files, the second to the Deacon assigned to the family, the third copy to the Finance Ministry for the assignment of an offering number and the original remains with the Intake Team Leader.

The New Member Intake Team Leader follows up with all new members with welcome telephone calls and invitations and subsequent reminders for them to attend Bible Study and Sunday School.

During intake, the new member is encouraged to signed up for New Members Orientation and encouraged to attend Sunday School and Bible Study.

How does one grow spiritually at your church?

Through the preaching and teaching of the word, worship, Sunday School and Bible Study.

How does your church encourage its members to reach people for Christ?

Through various outreach strategies.

How does a member get to serve Christ at your church?

By completing New Members Orientation, taking a Spiritual Gifts Assessment Profile to determine their spiritual gifts and completing the leadership track.

How does your church encourage its members to move to greater levels of commitment?

Through the proclamation of the Word, Bible Study, Sunday School and other specialized training.

What are the designated entry points at your church for a person to join Christ?

Worship
Bible Study

Sunday School
Specialized Events i.e. Vacation Bible School, Block Parties, Conferences

How do you believe God works in the lives of the members at your church?

God works through prayer and when disciples allow the preached and taught word to transform their lives. The practical application of living a transparent life that sets a godly example throughout the church and community.

What is your church's strategy to assimilate new member and new believers?

Encouraging members to complete New Members Orientation, discovering what their gifts are and participating by attending the leadership tracks. Members are encouraged to grow in Christ, serve Christ and reach others for Christ. To do this effectively, new members must be assimilated through the following process.

DNA 101

To orientate people to Christ and church membership. Developing the Disciple 202

To assist the disciple to spiritual maturity. Developing the Leader 303

Equipping emerging leaders with the skills they need to do ministry effectively.

Discovering Prospects for the Kingdom 404

To train and enlist people to share Christ and reach people for the kingdom.

Level 1: DNA (1 Session)

Level 2: Understanding Your Faith/Doctrine (2 Sessions) Spiritual Gifts (1 Session)

Becoming A Good Steward (1 Session) Reflections

Level 3: Leadership Development

Level 4: Reaching People for Christ

Take some time and work on your church's process

1. Your church's process

_____ >>> _____ >>> _____ >> _____

2. How do the weekly programs fit into the process?

_____

_____

_____

3. How does your Church illustrate the process?

_____

_____

_____

4. How does your church measure each stage of the process?

5. How does your church move members through the process?

_____

_____

_____

6. How does your church place its members in the pathway of God's transforming power?

_____

_____

_____

7. Is the process of your church designed to partner with God?

_____

_____

_____

8. What happens when a person joins the Body of Christ at your church?

_____

_____

_____

9. How does one grow spiritually at your church?

_____

_____

_____

10. How does your church encourage its members to reach people for Christ?

_____

_____

_____

11. How does a member get to serve Christ at your church?

_____

_____

_____

12. How does your church encourage its members to move to greater levels of commitment?

_____

_____

_____

13. What are the designated entry points at your church for a person to join Christ at your church?

    a. _____

    b. _____

    c. _____

    d. _____

14. How do you believe God works in the lives of the members at your church?

_____

_____

_____

15. What is your church's strategy to assimilate new member and new believers?

_____

_____

_____

CHAPTER EIGHT

Develop An Intentional Strategy

Your program should be designed with the knowledge of your unique community coupled with the gifts and resources of your church. There should be a strategy in place to reach the community.

The Five Essential Components of Strategy

1. ***Discover prospects.*** *The church must discover those who are prospects for the Gospel and then create avenues to reach them. You may try avenues such as personal invitation, seeking out new residents in the community, contacting persons who have recently attended your church.*
2. ***Train members*** *to present the Gospel in the power of the Holy Spirit.*
3. ***Take the Good News*** *to your community. Jesus expected Christians to take the message to the lost world. The evangelistic church will use every means possible to reach the lost. As a result of a church's commitment, to evangelize the un-church in any church service is an opportunity not to be overlooked.*
4. ***Challenge the lost*** *to commit to Christ.*
5. ***Assimilate*** *new members into the church body and nurtured to maturity.*

DEVELOP A PERSONALIZED STRATEGY

1. Effective outreach is typically a combination of several factors. Successful churches do not rely on a single method for reaching people; they use multiple strategies. Be creative!
2. Learn all you can about the people you are trying to reach. Gather demographic information to assist you in increasing your knowledge in the community. Venture out and meet the people of your community. Talk with the residents; determine what their needs and aspirations are.
3. Develop a presence in the community. Let people know your church exists. Consider sponsoring a community event. It's a great practice not to just simply invite people to come to you, but for your church to be a part of the community. Christians should be trained to see every community relationship as an opportunity for winning someone to Christ. Look for unique possibilities to develop presence.
4. Develop a regular visitation night. Organized visitation should be a part of the total outreach program of the church. Below are a few reasons a visitation program is effective; A Visitation program helps to create the evangelistic atmosphere develops a team spirit.

➤ creates an atmosphere of personal accountability.

➤ gives the participants a vision for supernatural activity.

➤ is an essential seed sowing activity that will enable you to realize an evangelistic harvest through other events.

➤ provides a training opportunity for teaching people to witness.

➤ will help sensitize your people to the actual needs that exist within the community.

5. Use events to discover prospects. Sponsor evangelistic events such as a musical presentation, block party celebration or special guest speaker helps to develop community presence.

6. Ministry-based outreach. Social ministries, which express no concern for the spiritual condition of individual, is incomplete. Evangelism, which displays no concern for the physical and social needs of people, presents a partial gospel. Evangelism provides a wonderful opportunity to meet needs and share the Gospel. Meeting needs opens the door of receptivity.

7. Schedule an outreach service. The keys are prayer and preparation, excellent pre-meeting planning, personal invitations to the lost, and a gifted evangelist. Make sure to schedule well in advance and follow through on necessary pre-meeting planning. Critical pre-meeting components often omitted are prospect discovery, evangelistic praying, and personal witnessing throughout the community.

8. Recruitment for outreach. As the church grows, the need increases for additional workers. Many churches consider recruiting volunteers, persons whose primary responsibility is outreach evangelism.

9. Budgeting for outreach. The church's budget will reflect its priorities. To be effective in reaching your community, you must provide the necessary resources.

10. Outreach is global and should be extended to the world. An evangelistic church cannot neglect the plight of the lost around the world. It should be involved in teaching missions, giving to missions, and challenging the people to do mission work around the world.

Activity

Take a few moments and do a mental survey of your community.

1. Determine who you are attempting to reach within the community.

_____

_____

2. What are you trying to accomplish among those that you reach?

_____

_____

3. What are you actively accomplishing within the community now?

_____

_____

4. List a few innovative evangelistic ideas/events your church can plan as a means of outreach in the community.

_____

_____

CHAPTER NINE

The Ministry Operating Plan

A Kingdom Focused Church

Your church should operate under the leadership of the Holy Spirit. Christ is the head of this body of believers. The church's foundation must be positioned as a kingdom focused church. What that means is, God shapes, molds and direct the path and structure of the church. It is not necessary for church leaders to run from seminar to seminar, program to program, workshop to workshop or even church to church to resolve how the church will function. To be successful, the focus of your church must come from the heart of God. The vision and purpose are given by God not from human intellect. A kingdom focused church exists to transform the unsaved and un-churched into mature Christians. With the intention of becoming committed disciples of Christ and disciple others, reproducing themselves.

An equipping church, builds Christians believers through worship, Sunday School, Bible Study and other specialized events. Upon joining the local church new believers must be turned over to the New Members Team. This team will ensure new members are assimilated through the church. Each member will be encouraged to complete the entire course of New Members Orientation (NMO).

It not recommended that new members be allowed to serve in any ministry or leadership capacity prior to completing NMO. This is to ensure they understand the church's vision its process and how the church carries out its purpose. Upon completion of NMO, new members will be introduced to the Christian Education (CEM) leader. The CEM leader will interview the member and assimilate them to the next step in their orientation journey.
The discovery of spiritual gifting will assist the member to determine where they fit in the ministry of the church. The results will be discussed with the member by the CEM leader. Training should be offered to accommodate the individuals to be equipped in their area of passion. At this point the member should have already completed their NMO.

Every person that will serve on any ministry team should be required to complete specialized training. This will enable the member to possess the knowledge and understanding of the ministry chosen. An example would be taking a teaching track or a leadership track, if they desired to serve in as a youth ministry facilitator. If a member senses a call to engage in a specific ministry, they may do so with the requirement that they are progressing through their ministry track. If a person does not complete their ministry track within one year of beginning the process, they should be required to resign from serving in any teaching ministry or leadership capacity. A member may serve in a ministry upon completion of NMO, but not in any leadership capacity. Once a member drops out of the specialized track, they will be required to start at the beginning of that class. Upon completion of their specialized training, members will advance to phase three, which is the Mobilization Phase.

Now the member is ready for mission and ministry. Each member is required to continue spiritual growth studies by enrolling into your church's ongoing Discipleship Development Program. Such as Sunday School and Bible Study. Every member should be committed to ongoing development as a Christian disciple. A Discipleship Development Program is an ongoing, organized study and interaction time where the member is encouraged to increase in the knowledge and application of Christian disciplines and principles.

A Servanthood Church

The church enlists, equip and train individuals to be servant leaders/deacons. Servant leaders/deacons are men and women who are committed to God, faithful to the ministry, and good stewards of God's resources. A servant leader/deacon will partner with the Pastor and the Chairman of Deacons or for a more contemporary title, the **Executive Servant Leader.** This role ensures that each family, within the church, is being properly ministered to and needs are met as they arise. A servant leader must first be called by God, and recruited by the pastor in collaboration with the Chairman of Deacons/ Executive Servant Leader. Each person chosen to become a servant leader must complete servant leader/deacon training. Upon completion of the required training, he or she will be commissioned to serve on the Servant Leader Team/Deaconate for a term of three years. Every servant/deacon must rotate off this team, for a period of no less than three years.

A Church of Decency and Order

Disorder must be dealt with swiftly with Christian love and truth. Order of any organization is critical to the effectiveness of that entity. For that reason, church discipline is valuable element for a healthy church. Any person causing factions, disturbing, or disrespecting the ministry of God, or His people, must be brought before the Pastor, the Chairman of Deacons/Executive Servant Leader, and a member at large which will make up the Decency and Order Team. This team will follow the Matthew 18 Model. If this person will not or cannot be reconciled, they must be excommunicated from serving on any ministry team in the church. The church family will continue to love this person and minister to them in an effort to assist them become a disciple of Christ. If the person continues to be disruptive in the body, he or she should be asked to leave the church.

A Ministry Team Church

One valued operational method for the church is when it profit from a ministry team concept instead of the traditional auxiliaries and committees. The ministry team concept is a more effective and efficient method of accomplishing the Great Commission. Each ministry has a team leader who is accountable and responsible to the Pastor. The team leader is not a boss, but someone that will assist and facilitate the team in accomplishing its mission according to the vision and purpose of the church. A team leader will serve a term of three years and rotate off, unless waived by the Pastor to serve an additional term, not to exceed six years. Every team leader must complete the required training in a leadership ministry track as well as being involved in Bible Study and Sunday School. Every team leader should sense the call of God to serve in the ministry they are chosen for.

A Church of Proper Business

Another nontraditional approach to church operations is to conduct business on a bi-annual basis during the months of June and December. This time together will consist of the church family coming together beginning with dinner, a time of prayer, worship and praise and the business at hand. The meeting will be facilitated by the Pastor and conducted according to Roberts Rule of Order, with the exception of voting. The church will come to a consensus rather than the traditional voting.

An Evangelistic Church

The church can discover innovative ways of reaching out to the community to advance the kingdom of God. This may be accomplished in various ways. {1} Brother to Brother Ministry, which is a men's ministry that will reach out to men by sponsoring various events for men and conducting men classes. {2} Sister to Sister Ministry that is designed to reach out to the women in the community and surrounding area, using the same approach as the Brother to Brother Ministry. {3} Specialized events, such as Upward Basketball. Upward Basketball is a program designed to reach youth and young adults through a basketball. {4} Each One Reach Ministry. Every member in the church invites and brings un-saved and un-church people to church. {5}FRAN-GELISM, this is an outreach ministry the church would have once or twice a year, where each member will invite on the; first Sunday, a friend. Second Sunday, a relative. Third Sunday, an acquaintance. Fourth Sunday, a neighbor.

CHAPTER TEN

Ministry Team Leaders

Ministry Team Leaders work together harmoniously with the Pastor, Chairman of Deacons/Executive Servant Leader to ensure the vision of the church is carried out decent and in order. The following is a brief synopsis of an outstanding leader.

The Task of Leadership

Spiritual leadership is the development of relationships with the people of a Christian organization or church body. With individuals and leadership teams formulated along with attaining biblically compatible goals that meet real needs. Spiritual leaders serve to motivate and empower others to achieve what otherwise couldn't be achieved unaccompanied.

Vision

A leader has greater vision than a manager. Leaders think future, beyond the day to day operational demands and immediate needs. This day-to-day mentality many times limits the vision of managers and followers. George Bernard Shaw said: "You see things; and you say, "Why?" But I dream of things that never were; and I say. "Why not?"
Leaders not only are dreamers but also inspire others to share in those dreams.

Renewal

Managers give directions and grade performance. Leaders, on the other hand, stimulate greater achievement and energize the entire organization. Leaders are more creative, innovative, and transforming than managers.

Orientation

Leaders are people-oriented; they constantly think in terms of their constituents and their needs. Managers tend to be more product and program oriented. Managers think more about getting jobs done. They focus on doing things to produce satisfactory results according to set criteria. Leaders, on the other hand, think about doing the right things to assist people maximize their potential.

Managers are conscious of efficiency, but leaders are conscious of values. Managers are quick to listen to people. A manager might say, "It can't be done," or "Maybe we can do it if . . ." a leader would say, *"We must find a way to do it, and we will." Managers supervise people, but leaders energize people.*

Leadership Strategies

There are five fundamental activities in the leader's task of spiritual empowerment.

1. ***Leaders Listen.*** Leaders must have a passionate desire to understand the hurts, longings, desires, temptations, sins, joys and real needs of groups and individuals that make up their ministry. Leadership involves effective communication and effective communication begins with listening.

    The counsel of the book of James should be remembered: "Dear brothers take note of this: Everyone should be quick to listen, slow to speak." Solomon shared his wisdom with us also: "Let the wise listen and add to their learning, and let the discerning get guidance . . . Listen to advice and accept instruction, and in the end you will be wise."

2. ***Leaders Build a Team.*** Persons, who build a solid sense of kinship, and cohesion between leaders and their ministry group, lead effective churches.

3. ***Leaders Inspire.*** If a spiritual leader wants others to acquire knowledge and be inspired, he/she must demonstrate worthwhile truths in his/her own life. Nothing leads as well as example. Values and morals are not transmitted easily by verbal or written methods. They are conveyed effectively by doing and doing visibly. "Follow me as I follow Christ" were the words Paul used to convey this, God's truth.

4. ***Leaders Focus on Values.*** Leaders focus on values, not machinery, programs or statistics. Poor leaders may give great attention to the details of running vacation Bible school, but they may have little knowledge of why all this is being done or what will be attained by it. Such persons may be good workers, but they are not leaders because they do not focus on causes, values and objectives. They see the details but not exactly how the program can meet basic needs and fuse into other activities of the church.

    Leadership that is busy doing unnecessary things is a problematic area for many churches. These type of leaders have no idea why these things are done except it is their custom. As a result of this mindset, many vital tasks are neglected due to this allegiance to tradition.

5. ***Leaders Balance Priorities.***

    There are three elements to effective church leadership:

    ➤ Personal (the individual)
    ➤ Social (the group)
    ➤ Production (the task)

LEADERSHIP AN AWESOME RESPONSIBILITY

The great spiritual leader is able to maintain focus on all three dimensions simultaneously, being careful to balance and assign equal weight and attention to each. They are skillful not to sacrifice any part of this triad to achieve one of the other components.

The task of the true spiritual leader is to promote growth in competence, responsibility, character, and leadership in individuals. They are committed to producing a healthy, functioning ministerial body. A spiritual leader promotes the achievement of the church's goals and plans in its community.

CHAPTER ELEVEN

The Church Leader In Partnership with God

Jesus explains himself in John, chapter 5, as confronts hostile religious leaders. He makes it clear to them, in the simplest terms, how he operates. He also knew, as He explained this to them, they would distort His words and would come after Him in an attempt to kill Him. This took power. Perhaps as much power as it took to heal the man at the pool of Bethesda. In other words, it takes the power of God to help us turn the other cheek, instead of trying to get even or take revenge. We must rely on the power of God to help us live above the scrutiny, beyond the scandal, clear of the backbiting, higher than the mean and vindictive ways of those against us as well ahead of the grip of those who simply don't like you. As leaders, serving in the kingdom of God, it is imperative we learn how to grasp the power of God and turn the other cheek. There will be many times, throughout your leadership sojourn, you will encounter difficult people. It truly takes the power of the living Christ to survive and thrive as a ministry leader.

What Jesus indicates in the text, is the secret of His power. His secret was that He is in partnership with God. When you are in partnership with the Most High, you too can operate out of a spirit of excellence.

Jesus' ministry was marked by the instantaneous power of God because He lived in continual partnership with the Father. Leaders not living and ministering in partnership with God, you will not experience the energy of our Creator working through their lives. Operating from a position of strength and might requires a life that is all encompassed by the Spirit. Ministry excellence is derived from this type of spirit-enveloped life. If you do not possess this power, your ministerial efforts will result in acceptable fruit instead of the exceptional fruit the Spirit demands.

In addition, to experience the fullness of God's blessing and power, leaders and their teams must walk in a spirit of excellence enabled through His perfect will. Most of the time, as leaders, we are walking in God's permissive state.

This means, on a personal level or within your ministry, you are living, choosing or serving in a manner that God is just tolerant of, not what or where He would specifically choose for you. This is not an optimum kingdom productive state for you or your ministry. Therefore, it is vital that we take Jesus' advice in verse John 5:30 . . ." I do not seek My own will but the will of the Father who sent Me."

Effective leaders seek God, to determine what His plan, His purpose, and His perfect will is. This is done in order to serve Him with a spirit of excellence! When any of these essential elements are neglected, you begin doing things on your own, in your own strength and according to your own emotions—not in the manner ministry should be accomplished. Because of this lapse, many leaders miss the mark and fall short of excellence.

First of all, to serve in a spirit of excellence we must be in partnership with God and bring to the table joint interest. This means our interest must be compatible with His.

> Then Jesus answered and said to them, "Most assuredly, I say to you, the Son can do nothing of Himself, but what He sees the Father do; for whatever He does, the Son also does in like manner." John 5:19

Everything God and Jesus accomplished was through joint interest. When you examine the word partnership, it means one who shares with another in some action or endeavor; having joint interest.

Jesus has a joint interest with God. What Jesus teaches us is to recognize the idiocy of self-sufficiency: "the Son can do nothing of His own accord." This is one of the leading problems within our lives and churches today, this operating in self-sufficiency. We are doing His work our apart from God. Many are serving, leading and ministering without God.

What the text implies is that we must be willing to be connected to the Father, in order to accomplish the purpose, in life He has predestined for us. Therefore, it would be a gross error to attempt to accomplish anything without God. Our every attempt to do my very best, without God, will still come up short. Jesus had a unique relationship with the Father.

There were no division, no friction between the Godhead. Any good partnership must have a unique relationship, there must be trust. Jesus trusted the Father and the Father could trust the son. Jesus did not try to do anything on His own.

You may be saying "It is hard for me to know God's perfect will." You are most likely correct. Firstly, it is difficult for us to take time to wait on God. Secondly, our love relationship with God is not where it should be. Therefore, many leaders are not totally connected to the Spirit of God.

Once you have an authentic, intimate relationship with God, He will reveal to you what He is doing. This leads to walking in His perfect will. In addition, when you are completely connected to the Spirit of the Lord, the Holy Spirit and the Word of God will instruct as well as assist you in recognizing God's perfect will. This vital connection enables you to serve in a spirit of excellence.

In spite of the availability of this valuable connection, we are still prone to the idiocy of self-sufficiency. Our tendency is to continue in the same patterns because of familiarity which equates to insanity; doing the same thing and expecting different results?

We tend to continue doing the same things, within the church, that our parents did yet expect different results. The results we achieve are repeated failings. A fruitful alternative would be to depend upon God to be at work in us and reveal to us what it is He wants done.

Self-sufficiency comes when you do things apart from God. It is virtually impossible for one to walk in a spirit of excellence without the Spirit of God. Jesus said He can do only what he sees his Father doing, because whatever the Father does the Son also does.

My mother would say from time to time, "you can climb on the top of "your high horse" aspiring to gain the admiration and attention of the world, "but if God is not in the picture your life will eventually go up in smoke."
Therefore, Jesus says I can't operate in the supernatural without God. Things won't fall into their proper place without God.

Not that it is physically impossible to function apart from the Father, for Jesus says that the Father has given Him power to act "out of Himself." Jesus could have created an entire universe anew. He had the power to do so. But the whole point of this is He chose never to exercise that power for His own benefit. When we are serving God within the church, it is improper to do so for your own benefit. If you serve with impure motives, you will always miss the mark and fall short.

Do you recall what happen in the wilderness when Jesus was tempted by the Devil to change stones into bread for his own satisfaction as well as to leap from the temple to gain the applause of people, or to gain the whole world for himself.

Jesus refused to fall into Satan's traps and temptations, for He knew who He was and realized that self-sufficiency would soon lead to self-destruction. Anytime we serve without God, we are bound to fail and fall. God gives His power to those who will not use it for their own benefit. "The Son can do nothing apart from the Father."

If we are going to serve in a spirit of excellence, there must be a partnership with God that brings to the table harmony

" . . . the Son can do nothing by Himself; He can do only what He sees His Father doing, because whatever the Father does the Son also does. He is looking at God the Father with an inner vision, and, seeing what the heart of the Father wants to do in a situation, He immediately obeys what is revealed to Him by the Father. Once again this can only take place when you are completely connected to the Spirit of God, in total harmony with God. The reason we are not serving God with a spirit of excellence, is most of time we are not completely connected to God. We are not in harmony with the Spirit of God. We are semi fleshly and partly spiritual.

One myou are praising and listening to God. The next moment, you are operating in the mode of self-sufficiency. When we take matters into your own hands, we push the partnership with God to side for a time, until we decide we desire to act more spiritual.

There has to be an inner connection within our spirit and the Holy Spirit in order for us to follow through with the things of God. Jesus knew what was desired of the Father because He was connected with the Father, tuned into the Spirit and recognized what God was doing in and around Him.

We must recognize that any effort made to operate apart from God and His power for our own benefit will finally leave nothing but a pile of mess; it will never accomplish anything. And we fail to serve in a spirit of excellence.

You cannot understand the truth of God unless the Spirit of God reveals it to you. If you don't have the Spirit of God, how can you serve with a spirit of excellence? Jesus said the Holy Spirit is our teacher. Yet, most of the time we do not pay attention to the teacher. Therefore, we continue to fail the specific areas of instruction God has us enrolled in.

When we pay close attention to our Master Teacher, He will teach us all things and lead us into all truth. It is critical to our increase that we sit before Him and learn from Him. We should study Him closely to see how He uses the Holy Scriptures to confirm the things of God within our hearts and reveal what God is doing all around us.

When this discipline becomes your habit, you will begin to hear God speaking as you pray and meditate upon the scriptures. God speaks, by the Holy Spirit, through His Word, prayer and situations around us. He reveals Himself, His purpose, and His ways. Are you in partnership with God?

Jesus lays before us the noteworthy example of being in partnership with God.

Jesus said "I can do nothing apart from the Father only what he sees the Father doing." Paul said in the third chapter of 2 Corinthians; "This is the confidence we have in Him, not as though there were anything coming from us, but everything coming from God. (Nothing from me, everything from God)," (2 Corinthians 3:4-6 RSV).

When you desire to walk in the perfect will of God and manifest the spirit of excellence, you will need to tap into the power of God. This will bring about the realization that nothing comes from you, but everything comes from God.

I cannot do anything apart from the Father that is true and lasting. We are in partnership with God. It is important to realize in and of ourselves, we cannot accomplish anything. In order to serve in a spirit of excellence, partnership brings to the table love for one another;

> "For the Father loves the Son, and shows Him all things that He Himself does; and He will show Him greater works than these that you may marvel."

The partnership within the Godhead is the unity of perfect love. This word love is phileo, the word for ordinary love; it is the love that denotes personal affection, brotherly love, and day to day down to earth love. It is homey love. This love allowed the Father to show the Son things He could not evidence to another. This enabled the Son to witness things no one else could see. Jesus looked at the man in need by the pool of Bethesda, and then looked to the Father. The Father looked at the Son, and then at the man in need. It did not matter whether it was the Sabbath or not, Jesus received the approval from the Father to heal.

When we are in sync with the Father, He will be able to reveal and unlock, to our understanding, many of life's mysteries directly to us. It is important for us to learn to look at the situations before us, then look to the Father for the power and understanding needed. It is then the Father will look at us, then to our situation and grant us the approval as well as power to do whatever it takes to rise up and walk.

Jesus helps us to understand what is behind this divine process of power and excellence.

It flows out of the Father's love for the Son. The "Father" whom Jesus is speaking to, is the Creator, the One whose brilliant mind conceived the glory of nature, the marvelous structures of life as well as the intricate blending and fitting together of the processes of the natural world. The Father "loves" the Son and delights to communicate to Him, in any given situation, the Father and the Son are in partnership together.

So it is with our partnership with the Son. He is the Lord of life, the Lord of nature, the Lord of the universe, the Lord of the nations, and He loves us. The writer of Hebrews says, "We do not yet see everything in subjection to him [man]. But we see

Jesus, who for a little while was made lower than the angels, crowned with glory and honor" . . ." (Hebrews 2:8b-9a).

Jesus says "the Father will show you greater works than these that you may marvel." Every manifestation of the Father's power (or the Son's power released in us), will awaken a sense of wonder on the part of those watching. A simple word, perhaps, a deed of compassion, a cup of cold water given to anyone in the name of the Lord, will leave an impact which causes people marvel. This is the result if we are operating through the power and Spirit of God.

Find out what God is doing in your life and around you and go in with Him. What does that mean? Well, it sounds like the words Jesus said in v 19. He could only do what he saw the father doing. He was in partnership with God. All of us must strive to be like Jesus, in partnership with the Father. The goal of our faith is to become more and more like Jesus. We need to be like him imitating the Father. Are you in partnership with God? Are you connected to the Spirit? Are you ready to find out where God is at work and join in with Him?

> *Yesterday is history. Tomorrow is a mystery. Today is a gift. That's why it's called, "the present."*
> *Unknown*

YOUR CHURCH'S PROCESS

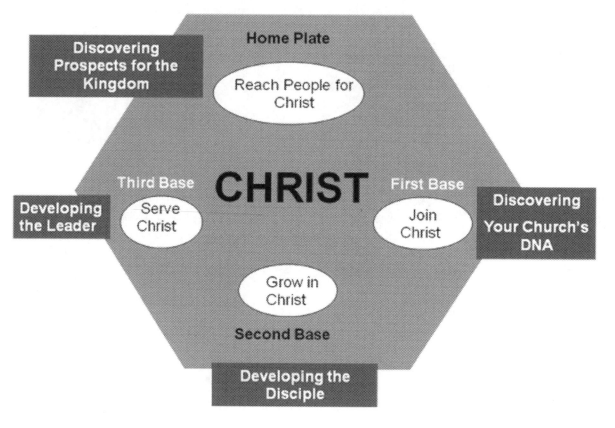

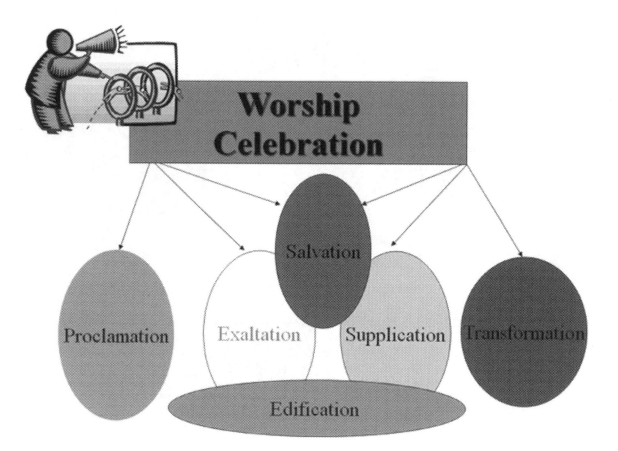

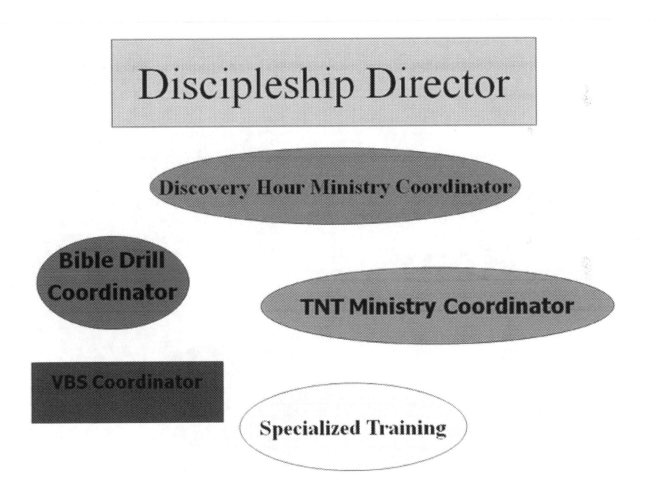

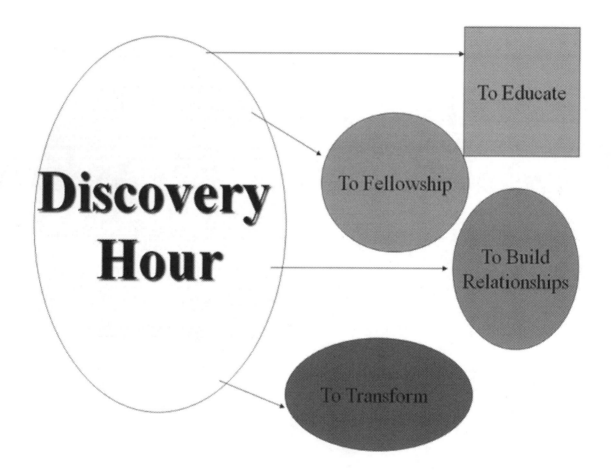

Fellowship Director

Hospitality Ministry Coordinator

Greeters

Event Planning

Fellowship Director

Hospitality Ministry Coordinator

Greeters

Event Planning

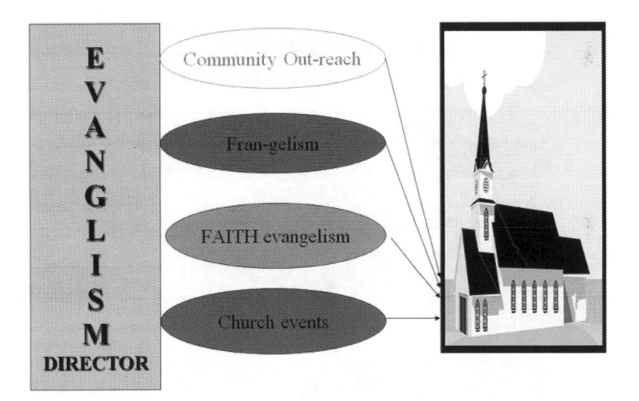

Worship Director

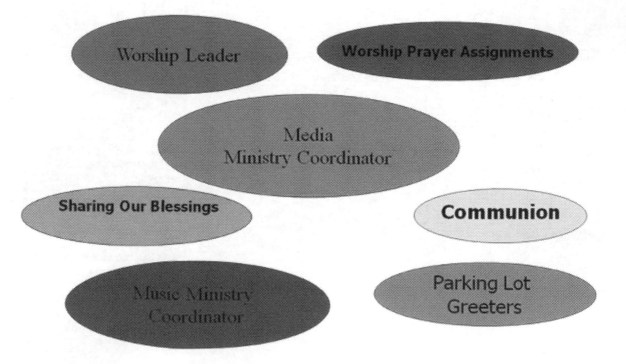

Worship Leader

Worship Prayer Assignments

Media
Ministry Coordinator

Sharing Our Blessings

Communion

Music Ministry
Coordinator

Parking Lot
Greeters

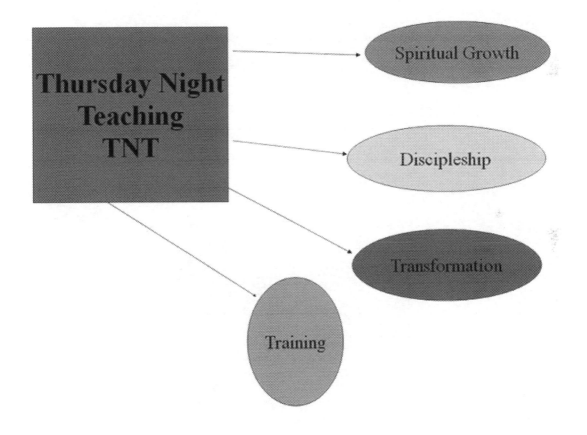

Youth Ministry

Collegiate
Ministry

Youth
Ministry

Preschool
Ministry

Children's
Ministry

Stewardship Director

This is a non-traditional structure layout. Remember to use an approach that best fits your particular ministry. Pray, seek God and follow the leadership of the Holy Spirit.

APPENDIX

Digging Deeper: My Inner Self

1. What ministries, groups of people or issues are important to me?

_____

_____

_____

2. What energizes me about Christ, church and ministry?

_____

_____

_____

3. What do I feel really passionate about?

_____

_____

_____

4. What consumes your thinking more than anything in regards to the kingdom of God?

_____

_____

_____

5. As you reflect on the above, what drives you more than anything? What are you most interested in?

_____

_____

_____

6. How can you channel what you have learned to make a greater difference in the kingdom of God?

My Leadership Vision Draft

_____

_____

_____

_____

_____

_____

_____

_____

My Leadership Mission Draft

_____

_____

_____

_____

_____

_____

_____

_____

My Core Values Draft

1. _____
2. _____
3. _____
4. _____
5. _____
6. _____
7. _____

My Motto

_____

_____

_____

_____

_____

"A Journey is not a trip, or a vacation.

It is a process and discovery of life."

Looking Ahead

Future Planning

Goal No. 1: _____

_____

_____

_____

Action Plan No. 1:_____

_____

_____

_____

Goal No. 2: _____

_____

_____

_____

Action Plan No. 2:_____

_____

_____

_____

MINISTRY RECAP SUMMARY

Ministry Title: _____ Report Month _____

Reported by: _____ Submission Date _____

MINISTRY INCIDENT SUMMARY

_____

_____

_____

_____

_____

_____

_____

MINISTRY NEEDS ASSESSMENT

_____

_____

_____

_____

_____

_____

_____

Submit to the Pastor or his designee by the 5th of each Month

BUDGET PROJECTION FORM

Ministry Title: _____ Contact Person _____

MAINTENANCE GOALS

Ministry Need/Event Description	Projected Amount	Approved Amount
1.		
2.		
3.		
4.		
5.		
6.		
Maintenance Ministry Total		

Financial support needed for year _____: $_____versus Financial support received previous year: $_____

NEW MINISTRY GOALS

Ministry Need/Event Description	Projected Amount	Approved Amount
1.		
2.	$	
3.	$	
4.	$	
New Ministry Goals Total	$	
TOTAL MINISTRY BUDGET REQUEST	$	

Budget Committee Review/Approval Date: _____

Pastor: _____ Business Manager: _____

BUDGET SUBMISSION FORM

Ministry Title: _____ Contact Person: _____

Ministry Mission: _____

_____

_____

MINISTRY EVENT/ACTIVITY	YTD _____ EXPENSES	20_____ BUDGET	20_____ PROJECTED EXPENSE	APPROVED AMOUNT
MINISTRY TOTALS				

Budget Team Review/Approval Date: _____ Pastor_____ Business Manager_____

Comments:

_____

_____